Summer Activities

Grow Your Brain

About Me!

Write your name.

_____

_____

Date

_____

Hey!
Paste your picture here!

Age?

Greatness!
In this oval, write something that is great about you!

_____

_____

_____

Where do you live?
Your city _____
Your state _____

Who is your best friend?
My best friend is:

_____

Top 5 Vacation Spots
List the top 5 places that you would like to visit.

_____

_____

_____

_____

_____

First to Second Grade

ISBN: 1-594413-23-1

PRINTED IN THE UNITED STATES OF AMERICA
10 9 8 7 6 5 4 3 2 1

What's Inside!

Hey Kids,

Can you believe that summer is already here? Think of all the time playing at the pool and hanging out at park, going to baseball games and staying up late, not to mention the family barbeques, Fourth of July fireworks, and of course spending all that time hanging out with your pals. But wait we need to add one more thing—this book!

With all the fun of summer, it's sometimes easy to forget that the new school year (sorry!) is waiting for us, and if summer is all play and no brain activity, then going back to school may not be nearly as fun as it should be!

So to help this be one of the most favorite, most exciting, most memorable summers on record, we came up with a really cool and easy way to help you remember all the great things you learned in reading, math, and writing last year so you are primed and ready to go on the first day of school next year! It's easy to use, and don't worry, we made sure that the activities are fun, interesting, and, of course, short! That way you will be done in no time and off to your next big adventure!

Have fun and enjoy everything you do this summer, and of course, remember to use your sunscreen, look out after your brothers and sisters, don't eat too many hot dogs at the barbecue, and above all, don't forget this book! Have a great summer!

The Cookie Jar Kids Club

How to Use  Summer Activities

  First, let your child explore the book. Flip through the pages and look at the activities with your child to help him/her become familiar with the book.

 Help select a good time for reading or working on the activities. Suggest a time before your child has played outside and becomes too tired to do their work.

 Provide any necessary materials. A pencil, ruler, eraser, and crayons are all that are required.

 Offer positive guidance. Children need a great deal of guidance. Remember, the activities are not meant to be tests. You want to create a relaxed and positive attitude toward learning. Work through at least one example on each page with your child. "Think aloud" and show your child how to solve problems.

 Give your child plenty of time to think. You may be surprised by how much children can do on their own.

 Stretch your child's thinking beyond the page. If you are reading a storybook, you might ask, "What do you think will happen next?" or "What would you do if this happened to you?" Encourage your child to name objects that begin with certain letters, or count the number of items in your shopping cart. Also, children often enjoy making up their own stories with illustrations.

 Reread stories and occasionally flip through completed pages. Completed pages and books will be a source of pride to your child and will help show how much he/she accomplished over the summer.

 Read and work on activities while outside. Take the workbook out in the backyard, to the park, or to a family campout. It can be fun wherever you are!

 Encourage siblings, babysitters, and neighborhood children to help with reading and activities. Other children are often perfect for providing the one-on-one attention necessary to reinforce reading skills.

Give plenty of approval! Stickers and stamps, or even a hand-drawn funny face are effective for recognizing a job well done. At the end of the summer, your child can feel proud of his/her accomplishments and will be eager for school to start.

Reading is the primary means to all learning. If a child cannot read effectively, other classroom subjects can remain out of reach.

You were probably the first person to introduce your child to the wonderful world of reading. As your child grows, it is important to continue encouraging his/her interest in reading to support the skills they are being taught in school.

This summer, make reading a priority in your household. Set aside time each day to read aloud to your child at bedtime or after lunch or dinner. Encourage your child take a break from playing, and stretch out with a book found on the **Summer Activities** Reading Book List. Choose a title that you have never read, or introduce your child to some of the books you enjoyed when you were their age! Books only seem to get better with time!

Visit the library to find books that meet your child's specific interests. Ask a librarian which books are popular among children of your child's grade. Take advantage of summer storytelling activities at the library. Ask the librarian about other resources, such as stories on cassette, compact disc, and the Internet.

Encourage reading in all settings and daily activities. Encourage your child to read house numbers, street signs, window banners, and packaging labels. Encourage your child to tell stories using pictures.

Best of all, show your child how much YOU like to read! Sit down with your child when he/she reads and enjoy a good book yourself. After dinner, share stories and ideas from newspapers and magazines that might interest your child. Make reading a way of life this summer!

Reading Book List

Ackerman, Karen
Song and Dance Man

Ahlberg, Janet
Funnybones

Allard, Harry
Miss Nelson Is Missing

Andersen, Hans Christian
(retold by Anne Rockwell)
The Emperor's New Clothes

Arnold, Tedd
No Jumping on the Bed

Brown, Marcia
Stone Soup: an Old Tale

Cohen, Barbara
Molly's Pilgrim

Cosgrove, Stephen
Leo the Lop—I, II, III
Hucklebug
Morgan and Me
Kartusch
Snaffles

Dicks, Terrance
Adventures of Goliath

Duvoisin, Roger
Petunia
Veronica

Freeman, Don
Corduroy

Grimm, Jacob
The Frog Prince

Hall, Donald
Ox-Cart Man

Hutchins, Pat
Don't Forget the Bacon!
Good Night Owl!
Rosie's Walk

Isadora, Rachel
My Ballet Class

Kellogg, Steven
Paul Bunyon, a Tall Tale

Leaf, Munro
The Story of Ferdinand
Wee Gillis

Lobel, Arnold
Frog and Toad series

McCaughrean, Geraldine
Saint George and the Dragon

McCloskey, Robert
Make Way for Ducklings

Minarik, Else Holmelund
Little Bear

Peet, Bill
The Ant and the Elephant
Big Bad Bruce
Buford, the Little Bighorn
The Caboose Who Got Loose
Jethro and Joel Were a Troll

Schwartz, Alvin
In a Dark, Dark Room

Sendak, Maurice
Higglety, Pigglety Pop!

Sharmat, Marjorie Weinman
Nate the Great and the
Musical Note

Slobodkina, Esphyr
Caps for Sale

Steig, William
Gorky Rises
Roland, the Minstrel Pig

Viorst, Judith
Alexander and the Terrible, Horrible,
No Good, Very Bad Day

Waber, Bernard
Ira Sleeps Over

Ward, Lynd
The Biggest Bear

Yolen, Jane
Picnic with Piggins

Ready for Reading

✔ Reading has been around for thousands of years and can open your mind to new ideas by making you think in different ways than television or radio!

✔ The more you read, the smarter you get!

Books I Have Finished Reading

Title	Author	Pages	Date Finished	Great	Evaluation Okay	Bad

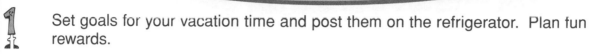
Try Something New
Fun Activity Ideas

1 Set goals for your vacation time and post them on the refrigerator. Plan fun rewards.

2 Visit your local library. Obtain a library card and check out a book.

3 Plant a garden.

4 Make designs on the sidewalk with water.

5 Go on a nature walk. Collect ten assorted bugs and leaves, and identify them.

6 Plan a reading picnic in the back yard, park, or canyon.

7 Do some stargazing tonight. Find the Big Dipper.

8 Have a neighborhood water fight.

9 Take a bus downtown with an adult and see a matinee movie.

10 Write a letter to a relative.

11 Go on a hike with a friend.

12 Surprise an elderly neighbor by weeding his or her garden.

13 Have a neighborhood baseball game.

14 Make up a play using old clothes as costumes.

15 Watch the sunset with your family.

Write to 100.

1	2			5					10
			14					19	
		23				27			
31				35					
	42						48		
					56				60
			64					69	
		73			76				
81									90
					96				

Circle the first letter underneath each picture if the picture begins with that sound. Circle the second letter if it ends with that sound. Color the pictures.

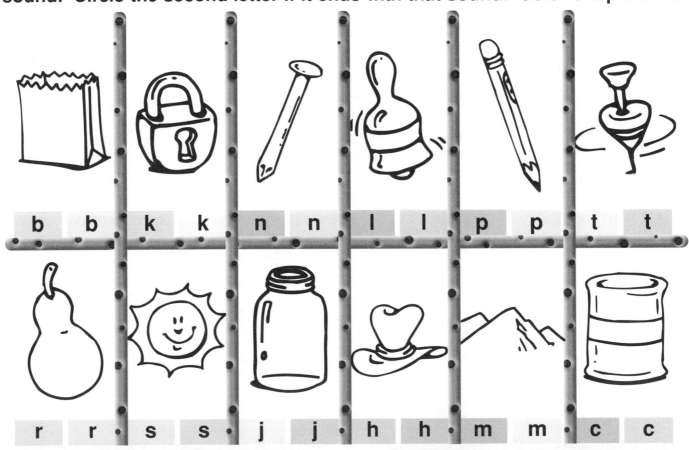

b	b	k	k	n	n	l	l	p	p	t	t

r	r	s	s	j	j	h	h	m	m	c	c

Write the capital letters of the alphabet.

EXAMPLE:

A B

Circle and write the correct word.

1. We will go in the _____.   van   can   ran

2. I can help the _____.   mat   man   tan

3. I am a good_____.   book   moon   cook

4. He is in his _____.   red   bed   fan

5. Can you get a _____?   the   it   book

6. I am a _____man.   sad   glass   sled

7. Find the big_____.   tug   pig   pink

8. Where is the _____?   hid   run   flag

9. I can run and _____.   jump   cup   went

10. I will take a hot _____.   moth   bath   tooth

COOKIE JAR PUBLISHING

Add or subtract.

3	4	5	2	0	8	1	7
+ 2	+ 3	+ 0	+ 1	+ 1	+ 1	+ 5	+ 2

	4	9	7	6	5	3	0	8
	- 2	- 3	- 7	- 4	- 1	- 2	- 0	- 5

9	0	3	8	4	7	5	5
- 4	+ 6	+ 5	+ 2	- 3	- 5	+ 5	- 3

Circle the first letter in the box below each picture if the picture begins with that sound. Circle the second letter if the picture ends with that sound. Color the pictures.

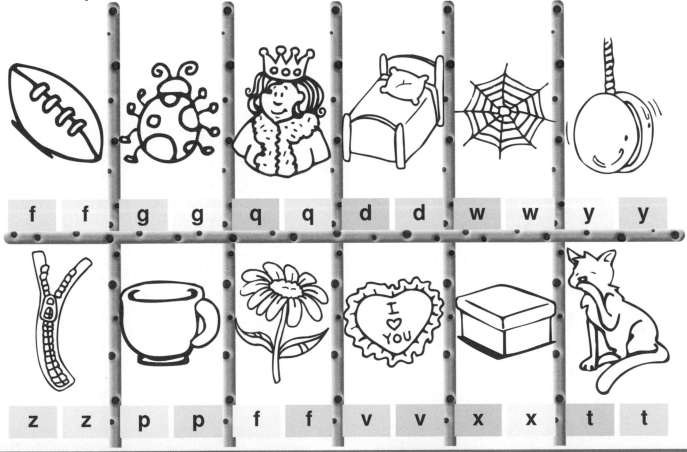

f	f	g	g	q	q	d	d	w	w	y	y

z	z	p	p	f	f	v	v	x	x	t	t

Write the lowercase letters of the alphabet.

EXAMPLE:

Practice reading these sentences. Draw a picture of your two favorite sentences.

1. The dog is stuck in the mud.
2. The cat will sit on Ann's lap.
3. The boy has a pet frog.
4. The man sat on his hat.
5. The hat is flat and smashed.
6. The rat ran on Sam's bed.
7. Sam is mad at the bad rat.
8. Fred met a girl with a wig.
9. The little bug bit the duck.
10. Fran had a pretty red dress.

Write the correct time on the small clocks. Draw hands on the big clocks.

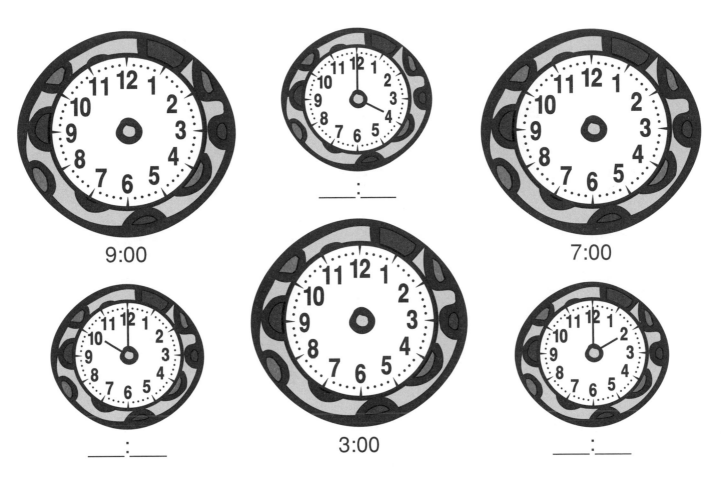

9:00

____:____

7:00

3:00

____:____

Write the long vowel sound next to each picture. Color the picture.

Match the sentence with the correct picture. Write the sentence number in the box.

1. The sun is very hot.
2. The ice cream truck is coming.
3. Dan and Trevor empty their bank.
4. Dan and Trevor lick their ice cream.

Draw and color pictures to go with these words.

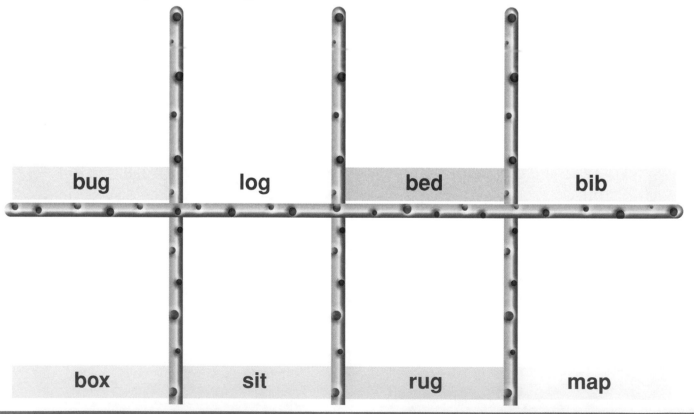

bug	log	bed	bib
box	sit	rug	map

Complete the counting pattern.

1   2   ___   ___   5   6   7   ___   ___   10   ___   ___

13   14   ___   16   ___   ___   19   ___   21   ___   ___   ___   24   ___

31   ___   ___   34   ___   36   ___   ___   ___   ___   40   41   ___   ___

44   ___   ___   47   ___   ___   50   ___   ___   53   ___   ___

___   ___   77   78   ___   ___   ___   82   ___   84   ___   ___   87

88   ___   ___   ___   92   ___   ___   ___   96   ___   ___   ___   100

Long and short vowels. Circle the correct word and color the picture.

| can | cane | can | cane | pin | pine | pin | pine | pane | pan | cap | cape |

| cub | cube | cub | cube | bite | bit | past | paste | rod | rode | not | note |

Practice writing your first and last name.

_____

- -

_____

- -

_____

- -

_____

- -

_____

- -

_____

- -

_____

End each sentence with the correct punctuation mark: (.), (!), or (?).

Is your pet fat_____

Do you like gum_____

Jan can blow bubbles_____

Can you jump a rope_____

The woman was mad_____

Are bears fuzzy_____

Babies cry a lot_____

Are clouds white_____

Where is your nose_____

Did he drop the box_____

Count the money and write in the amount.

 penny
1¢

 nickel
5¢

 dime
10¢

 quarter
25¢

    _____¢

    _____¢

    _____¢

   _____¢

    _____¢

Color the short vowel pictures blue and the long vowel pictures green.

Circle words that rhyme with the first word.

1.	**cat**	hat	ham	fat	pig	bat	rat	sat
2.	**bag**	rag	tag	dog	lag	nag	big	sag
3.	**he**	she	me	we	go	see	be	tree
4.	**cake**	rake	late	lake	make	bake	stake	said
5.	**bank**	sank	drank	pink	sunk	tank	prank	rack
6.	**sing**	ring	song	thing	wing	bring	sting	big
7.	**run**	fun	gum	gun	sun	bun	spun	tin
8.	**coat**	moon	boat	goat	joke	shout	float	moat
9.	**look**	took	shoot	book	cook	rock	boost	hook
10.	**seat**	neat	wheat	treat	sleep	beat	sled	leap

Follow these directions and color your picture.

1. Draw a tree.
2. Put a bird in your tree.
3. Draw a flower.
4. Draw a boy and his dog.
5. Draw a girl on a rock.
6. Give your picture a title.

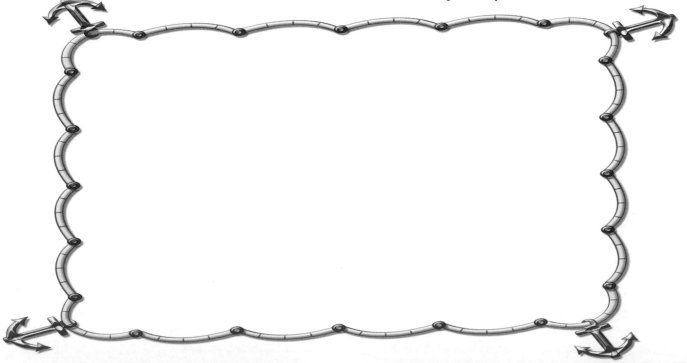

Count tens and ones.

EXAMPLE:
EXAMPLE:

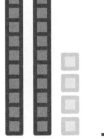

_____ 24

_____

_____

 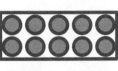 

_____

_____

_____

_____

Write the short vowel below the picture.

EXAMPLE:

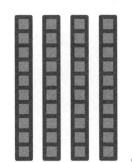

o
_____

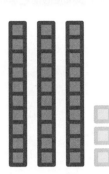

_____

_____

_____

_____

_____

_____

_____

Draw a line between the opposites.

EXAMPLE

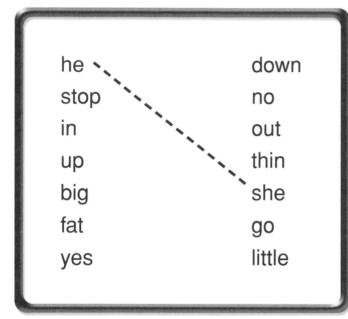

he	down
stop	no
in	out
up	thin
big	she
fat	go
yes	little

soft	clean
hot	slow
fast	cold
left	hard
off	bottom
dirty	right
top	on

Circle "yes" or "no." Draw a picture of your favorite sentence.

1. Can a car jump?   **yes**   **no**
2. Can a rug be wet?   **yes**   **no**
3. Can men skip?   **yes**   **no**
4. Is a kitten a baby cat?   **yes**   **no**
5. Do fish have fins?   **yes**   **no**
6. Can feet hop and run?   **yes**   **no**
7. Do rocks need sleep?   **yes**   **no**
8. Can hats fly?   **yes**   **no**
9. Do cows give milk?   **yes**   **no**
10. Can a leg be sore?   **yes**   **no**
11. Can a baby cry?   **yes**   **no**
12. Can a boy sing?   **yes**   **no**
13. Can a bear swim?   **yes**   **no**
14. Can a cow eat a lot?   **yes**   **no**

Read and answer these math problems.

1. Griffin has two green cars and eight red cars in his train. How many cars does Griffin have in all?

_____ green cars _____ red cars _____ cars in train

2. There were five birds in one nest. Then two birds flew away. How many birds were left in the nest?

_____ – _____ = _____

3. Matt had nine spelling words. He missed two words. How many words did he get right?

9 – 2 = _____

For each set of words, write the contraction in the word blank.

1. it is    it's

4. we will   _____

2. you will   _____

5. they have   _____

3. I am   _____

6. he will   _____

we'll   It's   you'll   I'm   he'll   they've

Draw a picture the color of the word.

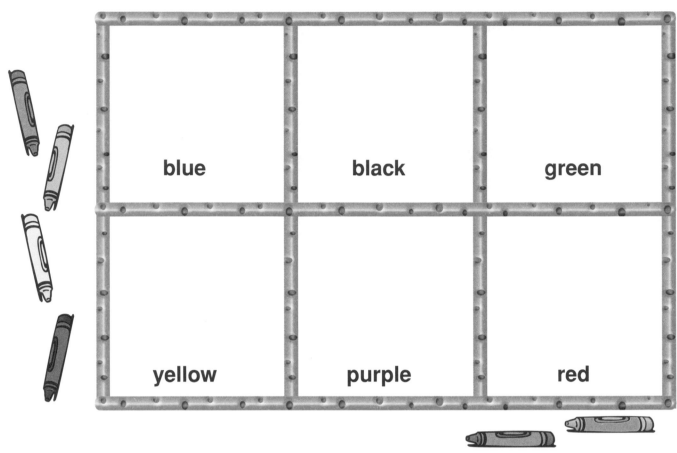

blue	black	green
yellow	purple	red

Circle the right word.

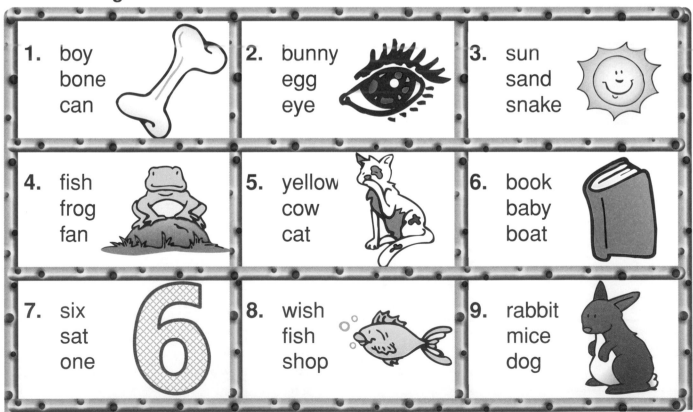

1. boy
   bone
   can

2. bunny
   egg
   eye

3. sun
   sand
   snake

4. fish
   frog
   fan

5. yellow
   cow
   cat

6. book
   baby
   boat

7. six
   sat
   one

8. wish
   fish
   shop

9. rabbit
   mice
   dog

Count the money and write in the amount.

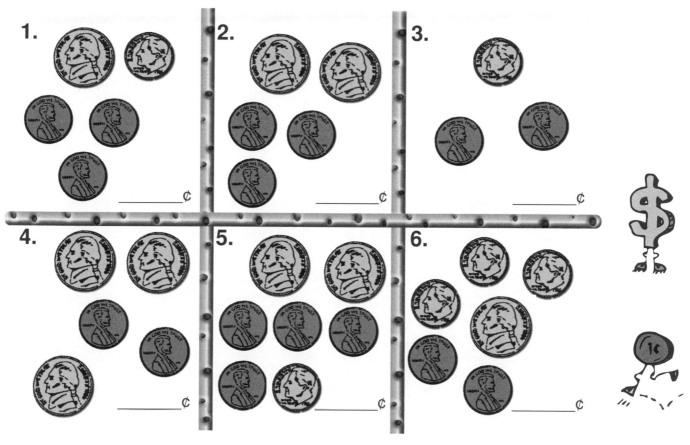

1. _____ ¢

2. _____ ¢

3. _____ ¢

4. _____ ¢

5. _____ ¢

6. _____ ¢

Write and finish this sentence in three different ways.
"I liked first grade because..."

1. _____

_____

2. _____

_____

3. _____

_____

In each sentence, draw a circle around the two words that rhyme. Color the picture.

1. The fish is in a dish.

2. The man in the boat is wearing a coat.

3. There is a bug in my mug.

4. The bee is in the tree.

Put the words in alphabetical order.

apple	1. _____	dog	1. _____
cat	2. _____	fish	2. _____
book	3. _____	elephant	3. _____

girl	1. _____	lamp	1. _____
ice	2. _____	king	2. _____
hat	3. _____	map	3. _____

hot	1. _____	well	1. _____
sit	2. _____	sleep	2. _____
cry	3. _____	dark	3. _____

Match the price of each toy with the correct amount of money.

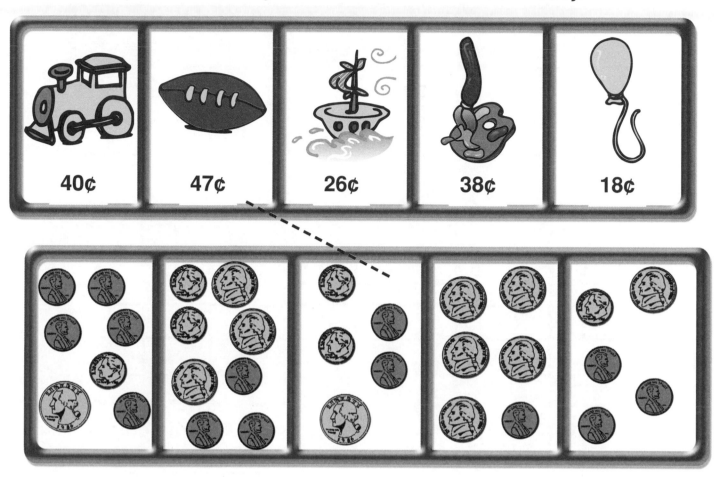

40¢   47¢   26¢   38¢   18¢

Find and circle the words.

I	F	L	Y	P	B	M	Y	W	C
D	C	C	M	I	D	T	A	I	L
E	F	E	H	E	I	I	G	L	I
H	I	G	H	G	M	E	U	D	M
N	I	G	H	T	E	I	Y	A	B

~~ice~~   wild   my   fly

pie   high   guy   dime

night   climb   tie   tail

Write the color words that fit in the boxes.

yellow   orange   blue   black   purple
green   brown   red   gray   pink   white

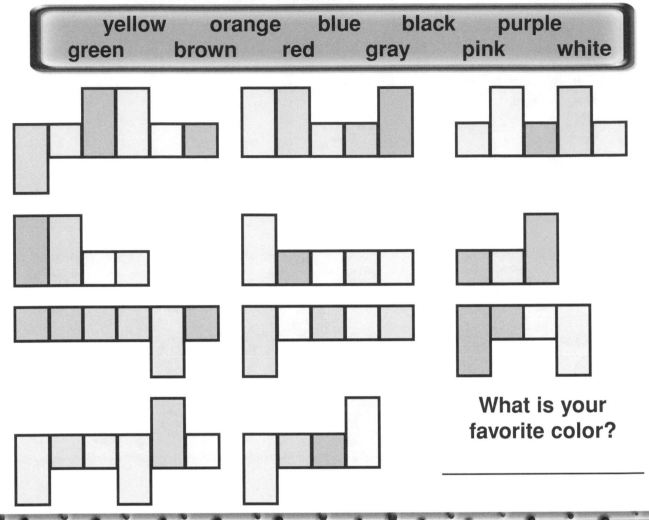

What is your favorite color?

_____

Put a (.) or a (?) at the end of each sentence. Draw a picture of your favorite sentence.

1. The dog ran down the road____

2. Do you like to play football____

3. Can a cat jump over a ditch____

4. We are going to school today____

5. What time do you go to bed____

6. Is green the color of a frog____

7. The farmer has ten horses____

8. Ann has a new blue dress____

9. We will walk to the store____

10. Will your mom go swimming with us____

Add or subtract.

5 + 6 = _____   6 + 4 = _____   3 + 8 = _____

7 + 3 = _____   9 - 5 = _____   6 - 4 = _____

10 + 1 = _____   8 - 3 = _____   2 + 9 = _____

8 - 2 = _____   10 - 4 = _____   9 - 3 = _____

10 - 5 = _____   8 + 2 = _____   9 + 3 = _____

6 + 5 = _____   7 + 4 = _____   8 + 0 = _____

Match each sentence with the correct job title.

EXAMpLE

I like to fish. - - - - - - - - - - - -   farmer

I deliver many things near and far.   pilot

I can stop traffic with one hand.   truck driver

I grow things to eat.   fisherman

I fly airplanes.   baker

I bake cakes and cookies.   policeman

Find the hidden picture. Color the long [ī] words in blue and the short (ĭ) words green. (The sound of [ī] can be in words with the letter [y], too.)

bib	fry	tie	light	my	sigh	try	wig
six	bike	sign	pie	guy	by	high	if
fib	gift	pit	dry	bite	miss	fish	lit
chin	sit	pill	time	night	hid	bill	quit
bin	mit	tin	cry	dime	win	fit	will
pin	fine	lie	sight	why	right	shy	fin
zip	ride	buy	side	hike	kite	nine	did

Something is wrong with one word in each sentence. Find the word and correct it!

1. Emily bocked a cake.

2. Ashley and i went to the zoo.

3. grant has a train.

4. Clean your toy rom.

5. Dan will ride hiz bike.

Complete the number families.

2, 3, 5   **2, 7, 9**   **3, 5, 8**

2 + 3 = ☐   7 + 2 = ☐   5 + 3 = ☐

3 + ☐ = 5   ☐ + 7 = 9   ☐ + ☐ = 8

5 - 2 = ☐   9 - ☐ = 2   8 - ☐ = ☐

☐ - 3 = 2   9 - ☐ = 7   ☐ - 3 = ☐

Circle the largest number in each set.

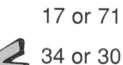

17 or 71   91 or 19   67 or 72

34 or 30   26 or 41   29 or 40

Read each puzzle. On the line, write a word that rhymes with the underlined word.

1. It rhymes with <u>mat</u>.
   It is something to love.
   It is a
   _____
   - - - - - - - - - - - - - - - -
   _____

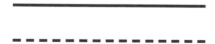

2. It rhymes with <u>boys</u>.
   Kids love to play with
   them. They are
   _____
   - - - - - - - - - - - - - - - -
   _____

Match the words to the right contraction.

EXAMPLE:

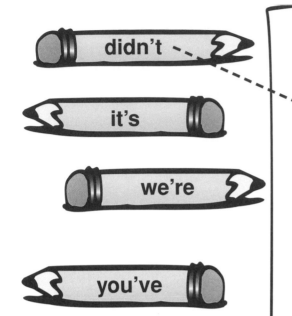

it is
we will
cannot
did not
we are
are not
you have
I have
do not
is not

Unscramble the sentences.

1. swim like Ducks to.

   _____

   -

   _____

2. pigs mud Do play in the?

   _____

   -

   _____

3. nests Birds in trees make.

   _____

   -

   _____

4. fun today Are having you?

   _____

   -

   _____

Add or Subtract.

8 + 2 = _____	10 - 4 = _____	2 + 1 = _____
4 + 4 = _____	5 - 2 = _____	7 - 3 = _____
3 + 7 = _____	6 - 3 = _____	5 - 4 = _____
1 + 9 = _____	4 - 4 = _____	10 - 5 = _____
3 + 3 = _____	7 - 4 = _____	3 + 2 = _____
6 + 4 = _____	3 - 1 = _____	5 + 4 = _____
5 + 2 = _____	9 - 4 = _____	6 - 2 = _____
10 + 0 = _____	8 - 3 = _____	4 + 4 = _____

Blends are two different consonants which join together to make a certain sound. Write the blends for the pictures below.

EXAMPLE:

d   r   _____   _____   _____   _____   _____   _____

_____   _____   _____   _____   _____   _____   _____   _____

Match the contractions with the word pairs. Write the answer on the line.

has _____ not

could _____ not

isn't
couldn't
hasn't
didn't

did _____ not

is _____ not

fuel

rub

huge

trunk

tube

cube

snug

Read the word on each balloon. If the word has a long (ū) sound, color the balloon yellow. If the word doesn't have a long (ū) sound, color the balloon any color but yellow.

Circle each problem that equals the number at the start of each row.

EXAMPLE

7	(3 + 4)	(9 - 2)	(5 + 2)	7 - 2	6 - 4	(7 + 0)	(8 - 1)
5	6 - 1	0 + 5	4 + 1	9 - 4	10 - 5	8 + 2	7 - 2
4	3 + 1	5 - 2	6 + 3	10 - 6	9 - 5	2 + 2	8 - 4
8	10 - 2	2 + 6	9 - 1	8 - 0	3 + 5	7 + 2	1 + 7
3	5 - 4	2 + 1	6 - 3	9 - 6	0 + 3	9 - 2	7 - 4
6	12 - 6	6 + 5	5 + 1	10 - 4	8 - 3	4 + 2	7 - 1

Find and circle the following words.

boy	bay	enjoy	say
joy	hay	toy	day

d	f	b	o	y	b	h	g	e
a	l	e	d	c	p	a	h	n
y	m	k	b	q	r	y	i	j
o	n	q	a	t	t	s	j	o
r	s	a	y	j	o	y	v	y
s	w	x	u	c	y	f	g	z

Combine the word and the picture to form a compound word.
Write it in the blank.

EXAMPLE

1.   cook   +   =   <u>cookbook</u>

2.   base   +   =   _____

3.      +   bell   =   _____

4.   life   +      =   _____

5.   [campfire picture]   +   fighter   =   _____

6.   cat   +   [fish picture]   =   _____

Put a 1, 2, or 3 in each box to show the right order.

☐ Emily ran into a rock with her bike.

☐ Emily and her bike tipped over.

☐ Emily went for a bike ride.

☐ Tim woke up and got out of bed.

☐ Tim rode the bus to school.

☐ Tim ate a big breakfast.

Complete the number families.

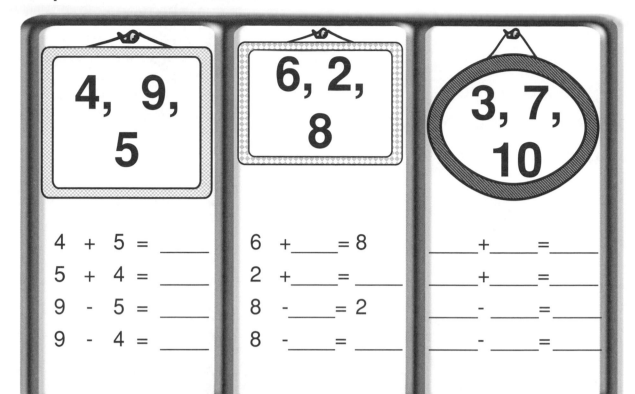

4, 9, 5

6, 2, 8

3, 7, 10

4 + 5 = _____
5 + 4 = _____
9 - 5 = _____
9 - 4 = _____

6 + _____ = 8
2 + _____ = _____
8 - _____ = 2
8 - _____ = _____

_____ + _____ = _____
_____ + _____ = _____
_____ - _____ = _____
_____ - _____ = _____

Write the beginning and ending sounds.

_____ e _____

_____ u _____

_____ u _____

_____ a _____

_____ e _____

_____ i _____

_____ o _____

_____ i _____

Circle the sentence that goes with the picture.

1. The girls fed the dogs.
2. The girls are afraid of the dogs.
3. The girls love the dogs.

1. Bob threw the baseball to his dad.
2. Bob threw the baseball to Ashley.
3. Bob threw the baseball to his mom.

Are the underlined words telling <u>who</u>, <u>what</u>, <u>when</u>, or <u>where</u>? Write the answer at the beginning of each sentence.

EXAMPLE

___who___ 1. <u>My mother</u> is going home.

_____ 2. We will go swimming <u>tomorrow morning</u>.

_____ 3. Children like to eat <u>candy</u>.

_____ 4. The ball is <u>under the bed</u>.

_____ 5. On the <u>Fourth of July</u>, my family and I will go on a picnic.

_____ 6. A big truck was stuck <u>in the mud</u>.

_____ 7. <u>Ashley and her friend</u> went on a trip.

_____ 8. The boy lost his <u>new skates</u> at the park.

_____ 9. <u>The clown</u> made everyone laugh.

Read and answer the math problems below. Write each problem.

1. The elves made four shoes the first night and six shoes the second night. How many shoes did they make?

_____ + _____ = _____

2. Tim had three balls. He found three more. How many balls does he have in all?

_____ + _____ = _____

3. A farmer had nine cows. He sold five of them. How many cows does he have left?

_____ - _____ = _____

Write the correct color words.

Snow is _____.

Grapes are _____.

The lettuce is _____.

The sun is _____.

My hat is _____.

Sam's dog is _____.

My friend's house is _____.

Tomatoes are _____.

Chocolate candy is _____.

Marshmallows are _____.

Teddy bears are _____.

The sky is _____.

Trees are _____.

My shoes are _____.

My eyes are _____.

My hair is _____.

Mud is _____.

Goldfish are _____.

Blackboards are _____.

Dad's car is _____.

Find and circle the words with the long vowel (ū) sound.

use	huge	glue	music
cube	cute	salute	tune

g	l	u	e	l	s	q	t	m
c	a	s	f	r	a	b	u	u
u	o	e	h	t	l	m	n	s
t	d	n	c	h	u	g	e	i
e	j	s	u	k	t	p	v	c
i	w	c	u	b	e	x	e	g

Check the box which best describes the picture.

☐ The mouse is in the box.

☐ The mouse is under the box.

☐ The mouse jumped out of the box.

☐ The bird is sleeping.

☐ The bird loves to sing.

☐ The bird never sings.

Words to Sound, Read, and Spell

short ă words

can	mad
cap	gas
fan	sad
lap	ax
man	bag
map	tax
ran	rag
nap	wax
bad	tag
tap	cab
dad	wag
yap	jab
had	gag
has	nab

short ĕ words

bet	fed
beg	vet
get	led
leg	set
jet	wed
peg	wet
let	hen
hem	yet
met	pen
pep	ten
net	
web	
bed	
yes	

short ĭ words

bit	him
bib	hip
fit	rim
rib	lip
mitt	bid
fib	sip
hit	hid
mix	rip
pit	kid
six	tip
quit	lid
fix	zip
sit	did
dim	quip
dip	rid

short ŏ words

dog	pop
ox	hot
fog	rod
box	lot
log	pod
fox	tot
jog	cot
mob	dot
hop	not
rob	got
mop	pot
sob	
top	
job	

short ŭ words

bug	sum
rut	rug
dug	gum
bun	tug
hug	bus
fun	lug
jug	tub
run	but
mud	sub
sun	cut
dud	rub
cup	nut
hum	cub
pup	
mum	
mug	

-ll words

bill	tell
fill	well
dill	yell
hill	bell
spill	fell
will	dull
quill	doll
sell	

-ss words

pass	kiss
mass	miss
boss	bliss
moss	fuss
toss	muss
loss	less
hiss	mess

-ck words

back	peck
pack	duck
dock	deck
quack	luck
lock	kick
rack	tuck
sock	lick
tack	pick
rock	sick
neck	quick
buck	wick

-ff words

buff	huff
cuff	puff

L- Blends to Read!

fl-	sl-	cl-	pl-	bl-	gl-
flat	slab	class	plan	black	glum
flag	slack	clap	plat	bled	glut
flap	slam	clam	pled	bless	gloss
fled	slap	click	plot	bliss	glass
flex	sled	cliff	plop	blob	glad
flick	slick	clip	pluck	block	glory
flip	slid	clock	plum	blot	glow
flock	slim	clog	plug	bluff	
floss	slip	club	plus		
flop	slot	cluck			
fluff	slug				
flux					

R- Blends to Read!

gr-		br-	fr-	dr-	tr-	cr-	pr-
grab	grill	brag	free	drag	track	crab	practice
grape	grip	brake	fret	drab	trap	crack	prince
grass	grog	brand	frill	dress	trick	crib	price
grid	grub	brass	frog	drill	trip	crick	pray
grim	gruff	brave	from	drip	trim	cross	praise
grin		brick	fry	drop	trot	crop	prairie
				drug	truck		present
				drum			

Look at the endings.

-mp		-st			-sk	-sp	-lf	-lk		-lp	-lt
camp	romp	cast	rest	last	mask	gasp	shelf	milk	silk	scalp	belt
lamp	chomp	best	fist	dust	task	clasp	golf	bulk		help	melt
ramp		fast	test	fast	disk	lisp		sulk		gulp	spilt
stamp		nest	lost	must	brisk	crisp		elk		pulp	quilt
limp		last	vest		dusk						
stomp		pest	cost		tusk						
bump		past	zest		desk						
dump		jest	frost								
jump		blast	chest								
pump		quest	past								
stump		list	bust								

Two sounds of (oo)!

1		2		
book	boo	doom	goose	
look	moo	broom	moose	
took	too	bloom	loose	
shook	zoo	groom	boot	
hook	moon	gloom	hoot	
cook	soon	cool	loot	
crook	noon	fool	root	
brook	spoon	tool	toot	
hood	food	pool	scoot	
wood	spook	spool	hoop	
hoof	boom	stool	loop	
stood	room	school		
foot	zoom	ooze		
wool				

Try these!

st-	sp-	sn-	sk-	sm-	sw-
stick	spud	snug	skip	smack	swag
stiff	spun	snub	skid	smell	swam
still	speck	snob	skit	smock	swim
stop	spell	sniff	skill	smog	Swiss
stock	sped	snip	skim	smug	swig
stab	span	snack			swell
stack	spat	snap			
staff	spill				
stag	spin				
stem	split				
step					

These vowels go walking and the first one does the talking!

oat	oak	toaster	blackboard
boat	soak	toast	dashboard
coat	cloak	coach	surfboard
float	croak	poach	skateboard
throat	soap	approach	scoreboard
load	oar	cockroach	steamboat
toad	roar	raincoat	railroad
road	foal	coatrack	roadrunner
roam	coal	foam	boast
moan	coast	groan	roast

Outline Yourself

Get a piece of butcher paper that is as long and as wide as you are. Lie down on it and have someone outline you with a marker. After, color in all the details — eyes, ears, mouth, clothes, arms, hands, etc. Hang it in your room and match yourself to it on the first day of school. Did you grow any during the summer?

Tree Generations

Make a tree rubbing by holding a piece of paper to the bark of a tree and gently rubbing a peeled crayon over it until the pattern of the bark shows through. Now make your own family tree. You can do this with names or pictures. Follow the example. Each generation is twice as big as the one before. This is how many people it took to make you!

Try Something New

Fun Activity Ideas

1. Decorate your bike. Have a neighborhood parade.

2. Catch a butterfly.

3. Get the neighborhood together and play hide-and-seek.

4. Take a tour of the local hospital.

5. Check on how your garden is doing.

6. Make snow cones with crushed ice and punch.

7. Go on a bike ride.

8. Run through the sprinklers.

9. Create a family symphony with bottles, pans, and rubber bands.

10. Collect sticks and mud. Build a bird's nest.

11. Help plan your family grocery list.

12. Go swimming with a friend.

13. Clean your bedroom and closet.

14. Go to the local zoo.

15. In the early morning, listen to the birds sing.

16. Make a cereal treat.

17. Read a story to a younger child.

18. Lie down on the grass and find shapes in the clouds.

19. Color noodles with food coloring. String them for a necklace or glue a design on paper.

20. Organize your toys.

Complete the counting patterns.

10	20		40			70			100

5	10	15				35	40		
55			70				90		

2	4		8		12			18		22
	26		32					42		

Write in the short and long vowels.

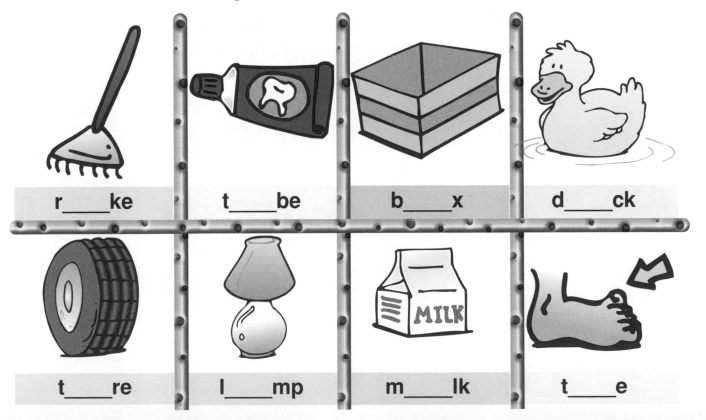

r____ke   t____be   b____x   d____ck

t____re   l____mp   m____lk   t____e

Hobbies

A hobby is something we enjoy doing in our spare time. Some children like to make things. Some like to collect things. Some play music and some do other fun things. Hobbies are fun. Do you have a hobby?

Draw and color a picture of one of your hobbies!

Catch each butterfly. Put each one in the right net by drawing a line to where it belongs.

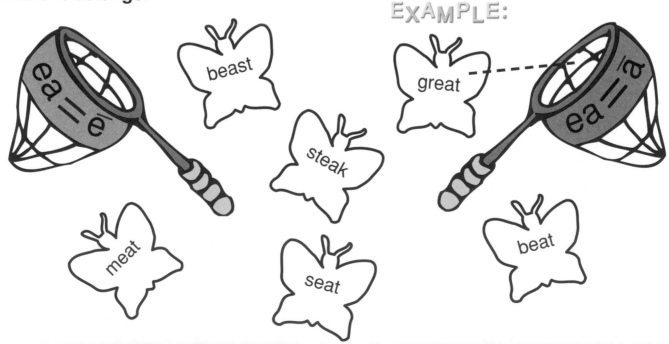

EXAMPLE:

Decide how many tens and how many ones make up each number.

EXAMPLE

26 = __2__ tens __6__ ones.   41 = _____ ones _____ tens.

45 = _____ tens _____ ones.   69 = _____ ones _____ tens.

65 = _____ ones _____ tens.   84 = _____ tens _____ ones.

17 = _____ ones _____ tens.   72 = _____ ones _____ tens.

50 = _____ tens _____ ones.   39 = _____ tens _____ ones.

97 = _____ ones _____ tens.   51 = _____ ones _____ tens.

35 = _____ tens _____ ones.   100 = _____ tens _____ ones.

Read the sentence, then follow the directions.

Ashley hugged her dog three times.

1. Circle the word "hugged."
2. Draw a box around the word that tells who Ashley hugged.
3. Underline the word that tells who hugged the dog.
4. Draw a picture of Ashley and her dog.

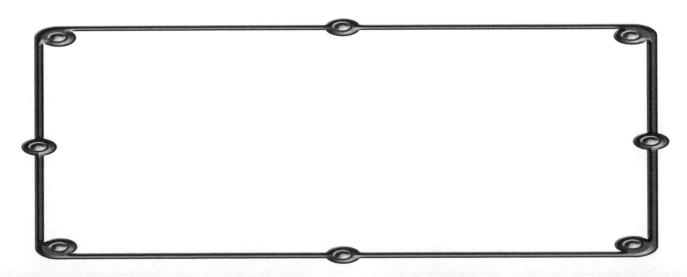

Number these sentences in the order they happened.

☐ The sun came out. It was a pretty day.

☐ The thunder roared and the lightning flashed.

☐ It rained and rained.

☐ Emily put her umbrella away.

☐ Emily walked under her umbrella.

☐ The clouds came and the sky was dark.

Finish the story.

Once there was a sun. The happy sun loved to shine its rays of brightness onto the earth because...

Draw the hands to match the time, or write the time to match the hands.

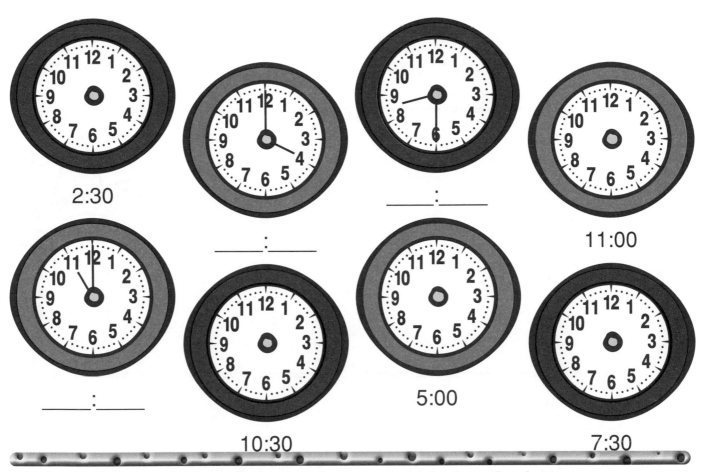

2:30

_____:_____

11:00

_____:_____

_____:_____

10:30

5:00

7:30

Circle the letters that spell the beginning sound of each picture.

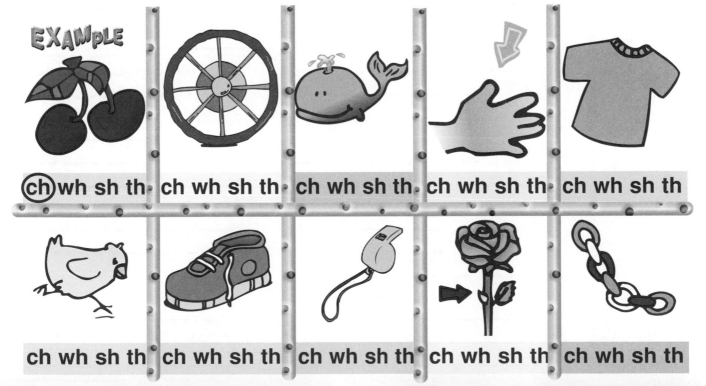

EXAMPLE

(ch) wh sh th | ch wh sh th | ch wh sh th | ch wh sh th | ch wh sh th

ch wh sh th | ch wh sh th | ch wh sh th | ch wh sh th | ch wh sh th

Read and decide.

One day, a man went on a hunt. He hunted for a long time. At the end of the day, he was very happy. What do you think the man found? Did he find something to eat? Did he find something pretty? Did he find something funny? Decide what the man found and draw a picture of it!

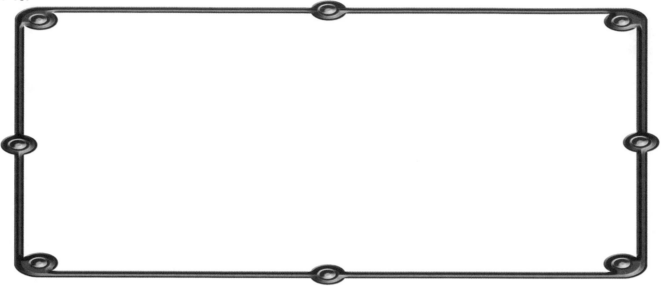

Put the following words in alphabetical order.

he
up
fat
little
big
stop
and
out
slow
go

1. _____

2. _____

3. _____

4. _____

5. _____

6. _____

7. _____

8. _____

9. _____

10. _____

Solve these problems.

1. Dan found five bees.
Ashley found five bees.
How many bees are there
in all?

+

_____ bees

2. Lisa has four fish.
Mike has six fish.
How many fish are
there in all?

+

_____ fish

**Word Study
and
Spelling List**

dime	make
name	plate
gave	size
nine	five
lake	bake
time	wise

Write the words with the long (ā) sound.

_____ _____ _____

_____ _____ _____

_____ _____ _____

Write the words with the long (ī) sound.

_____ _____ _____

_____ _____ _____

_____ _____ _____

Read each story. Choose the best title.

Travis is up now. He hits the ball. "Run, Travis, run! Run to first base, then to second. Can you run to home base?"

1. Running   2. Travis Plays
3. Travis's Baseball Game

 A rabbit can jump. Frogs can jump too—but a kangaroo is the best jumper of all!

1. Jumping Rabbits
2. Animals That Jump
3. Hop! Hop! Hop!

Emily put on her blue coat and her fuzzy, pink hat. Then she put on her warm, white mittens.

1. A Hot Day
2. Getting Ready to Go
3. Emily Likes to Play

Dan gave his pet dog a bone. He gave his fat cat some canned cat food. He also fed the ducks.

1. Feeding the Animals
2. Dan's Animals
3. Cats, Dogs, and Birds

Make these words plural, meaning more than one, by adding -s or -es.

1. cat _____
2. glass _____
3. truck _____
4. fan _____
5. wish _____
6. ball _____
7. box _____
8. bird _____

9. kitten _____
10. inch _____
11. dish _____
12. clock _____
13. bus _____
14. peach _____
15. brush _____
16. dog _____

Subtract and fill in the answers on the outer circle.

EXAMPLE

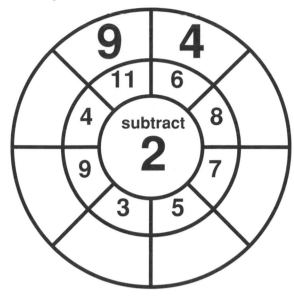

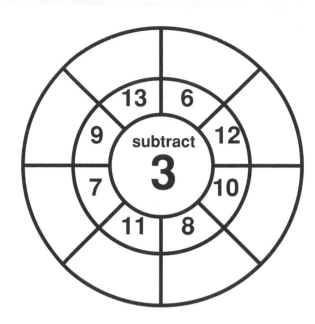

Circle and write the word that goes with each picture.

glove

glue

flower

flag

flashlight

fly

Use the following words to fill in the blanks:

Who	What	Where	Why	When

1. _____ are my keys?

2. _____ funny toy is mine?

3. _____ is your birthday party?

4. _____ is Mother coming?

5. _____ was there?

6. _____ is the sky dark?

Draw the other half. Color.

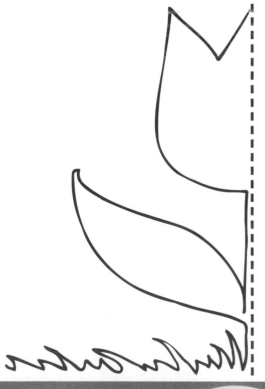

Solve the following problems.

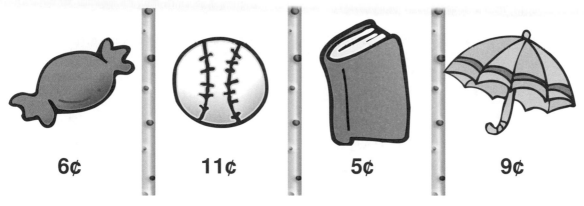

6¢	11¢	5¢	9¢

EXAMPLE

Lisa has 15¢. She bought an

```
  15
-  9
─────
  6¢
```

How much does she have left?

Griffin bought a and a

How much did he spend?

[ ]
[ ]
─────
[ ]

Emily has 12¢. She bought a

[ ]
[ ]
─────
[ ]

How much does she have left?

Trevor bought a and a

How much did he spend?

[ ]
[ ]
─────
[ ]

What month comes next? Fill in the blanks.

January	February	
April		June
		September
	November	

How many months are in a year? _____

Write the correct word on each line.

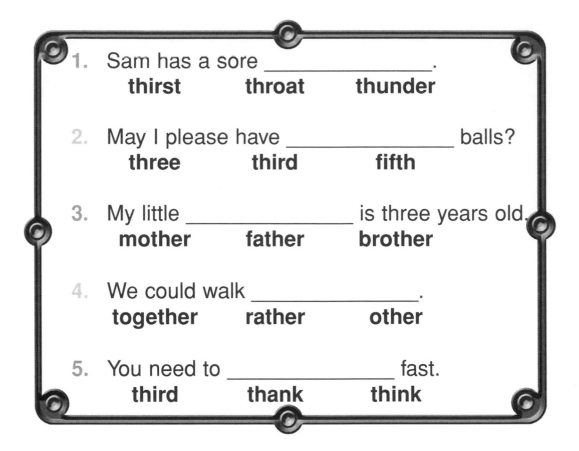

1. Sam has a sore _____.
   thirst   **throat**   **thunder**

2. May I please have _____ balls?
   three   **third**   **fifth**

3. My little _____ is three years old.
   mother   **father**   **brother**

4. We could walk _____.
   together   **rather**   **other**

5. You need to _____ fast.
   third   **thank**   **think**

Finish the story.

Last night I had the strangest dream. I dreamed that I...

Do a survey with your family and friends to see which flavor of popsicle is the most popular.

_____root beer   _____lime

_____orange   _____cherry

_____banana   _____grape

              _____(others not listed)

Graph the results of your survey by placing an X on the coordinates of flavors and the number of people who liked them.

Root Beer																				
Orange																				
Banana																				
Lime																				
Cherry																				
Grape																				
Other																				
	1	2	3	4	5	6	7	8	9	10	11	12	13	14	15	16	17	18	19	20

What is your favorite flavor?   Which flavor was the least popular?

_____   _____

Which flavor was the most popular?

_____

Read, study, and spell.

1.	bake	bakes	baking	baked	baker
2.	walk	walks	walking	walked	walker
3.	stop	stops	stopping	stopped	stopper
4.	mix	mixes	mixing	mixed	mixer
5.	listen	listens	listening	listened	listener
6.	plant	plants	planting	planted	planter
7.	call	calls	calling	called	caller
8.	hug	hugs	hugging	hugged	hugger

Read the story, then answer the questions below.

Mike lives on a farm. He wakes up early to do chores. Mike feeds the horses and pigs. He also collects the eggs. Sometimes, he helps his dad milk the cows. His favorite thing to do in the morning is eat breakfast.

1. Where does Mike live? _____

2. Why does he have to wake up early? _____

3. Name one chore Mike has to do: _____

4. What is his favorite thing to do in the morning?

_____

Answer the puzzle below. Color each picture the color below its space.

oi

c____ ____n   v____ ____ce   ____ ____l

_____ You can put this in your pocket.
yellow

_____ You use this to hum, talk, and laugh.
green

_____ Put this on and no more squeaks!
red

Add.

1.

2	1	4	5	2	4	5	3	8
2	1	4	5	3	3	4	5	0
+2	+1	+4	+5	+2	+0	+5	+3	+2

2.

3	6	7	10	8	5	9	2	4
3	6	0	10	3	1	0	3	4
+3	+6	+7	+10	+2	+5	+1	+7	+3

Give some facts about you and your family. Draw a picture of your family.

1. I live in _____.
2. I have _____ sisters.
3. I have _____ brothers.
4. My mom's name is _____.
5. My dad's name is _____.

6. This summer we are going to _____.
7. I am _____ years old.
8. We have a pet _____.
9. My favorite food is _____.
10. My favorite color is _____.

What day comes next? Fill in the blanks.

Sunday,_____, _____,
Wednesday, _____, Friday, and
_____.

How many days are in a week? _____

Name the days you go to school during the week.

_____, _____,

_____, _____,

_____.

Complete these sentences by unscrambling the words and writing them in the blanks.

1. Mike had a _____ for _____ mother.
   igft　　　　　　　**ihs**

2. The _____ has a broken window.
   acr

3. A bee _____ on _____ flower.
   ats　　　　　　　**hte**

4. My _____ works at the _____.
   add　　　　　　　**tsoer**

5. Sue _____ a _____ dog named Spot.
   sha　　　　　**ept**

Add.

5	8	3	9	15	10	8	9	6
+7	+4	+7	+5	+2	+6	+3	+4	+5

Subtract.

12	9	11	8	10	6	7	12	10
-8	-4	-7	-8	-2	-2	-5	-4	-6

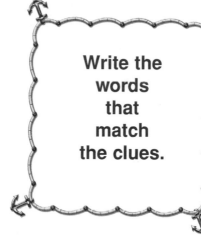

Write the words that match the clues.

EXAMPLE

1. It begins like stuck. It rhymes with <u>late</u>.

   _____ state _____

2. It begins like rip. It rhymes with <u>cake</u>.

   _____

3. It begins like very. It rhymes with <u>note</u>. _____

4. It begins like break. It rhymes with <u>him</u>. _____

5. It begins like gum. It rhymes with <u>late</u>. _____

6. It begins like trip. It rhymes with <u>rim</u>. _____

Read the story below and then answer the questions.

Ashley has a box of peaches. She wants to take the peaches home to her mother, so her mother can make a peach pie. Ashley says, "I love to eat peach pie!"

1. Who has a box of peaches?_____

2. Who does she want to take the peaches to? _____

3. What does she want her mother to make? _____

4. Ashley says, "I love to eat _____!"

Complete the phrase below. Write at least three complete sentences.

I like myself because I can…

_____

_____

_____

_____

_____

_____

_____

_____

_____

_____

_____

Write the numeral by the number word.

_____ six	_____ nine	_____ four	_____ seven
_____ ten	_____ two	_____ three	_____ one
_____ five	_____ eight	_____ zero	_____ twelve

_____ nineteen	_____ eleven	_____ fourteen
_____ twenty-one	_____ sixteen	_____ eighteen
_____ thirteen	_____ fifteen	_____ seventeen
_____ twenty	_____ twenty-five	_____ thirty

Does the (y) say (ī) or (ē) in the words below?
Write (i) or (e) in the boxes.

ī or ē

☐	☐	☐	☐	☐	☐
baby	fly	windy	bunny	fry	cherry

☐	☐	☐	☐	☐	☐
shy	family	silly	happy	jelly	pony

☐	☐	☐	☐	☐	☐
cry	my	funny	buy	try	candy

Draw the following.

1. Draw one tree.
2. Draw four flowers.
3. Color one orange butterfly in the tree.
4. Draw a park bench.
5. Draw three pigeons beside the bench.
6. Draw a yellow sun.

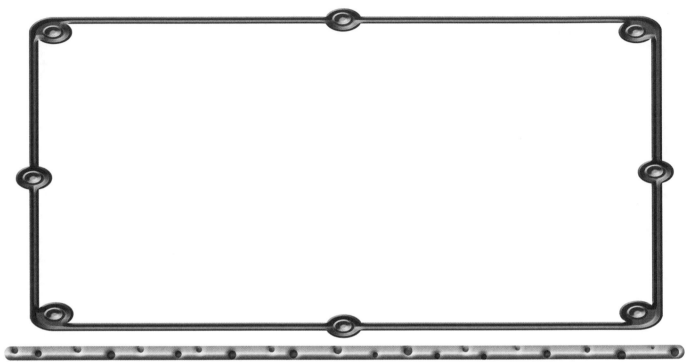

Read the story, then answer the questions.

Sam is excited for summer. He wants to do many things. He wants to visit all of the animals at the zoo. He also wants to go camping in the mountains. Sam loves to swim and play with his friends, too.

1. What is Sam excited for? _____
2. What does he want to visit at the zoo? _____
3. Where does he want to go camping? _____
4. What does Sam love to do? _____

   and _____

Use the problems below to work on place value. Be sure to read before you write.

46 = _____ tens _____ ones

19 = _____ ones _____ tens

84 = _____ tens _____ ones

64 = _____ tens _____ ones

7 tens and 6 ones =

4 tens and 0 ones =

1 ten and 1 one   =

9 ones and 3 tens =

1 hundred, 2 tens, and 8 ones = _____

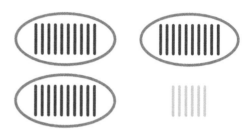

_____

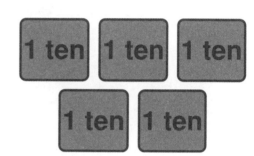

_____

10 **10** 1 1

_____

Circle the root or base word in each of the following words.

1. (run)ning
2. hopped
3. fastest
4. standing
5. ripped
6. tallest
7. digging
8. slowly

9. playful
10. boxes
11. lovely
12. sickness
13. stepping
14. careful
15. dropped
16. catches

17. friendly
18. rabbits
19. starry
20. mopped
21. sadness
22. missing
23. bigger
24. mixed

COOKIE JAR PUBLISHING

Fill in the circle in front of each correct answer. There may be more than one correct answer in each box.

We can smell	**We can feel**	**We can see**	**We can taste**
O cakes in the oven.	O the cold rain.	O a sweater on the shelf.	O the porch swing.
O cookies on a plate.	O sand on the seashore.	O a pain in our leg.	O a green apple.
O wind blowing the trees.	O the night.	O a watch on a chain.	O a cheese sandwich.

We can feel	**We can see**	**We can taste**	**We can smell**
O the hot sunshine.	O soldiers marching.	O a dill pickle.	O a rose on a bush.
O a cold dish.	O the weeks.	O popcorn in a dish.	O the ticking of a clock.
O the dog chasing a cat.	O a scratch on the table.	O a cloud in the sky.	O dinner cooking.

If you planted a garden, what would you plant and why? Draw a picture.

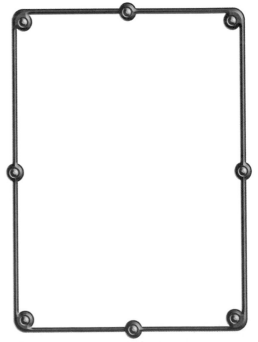

Solve these problems.

Trevor spent 8¢.
Ashley spent 2¢.
How much did they
spend together?

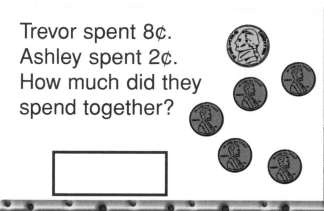

Emily has 10 bows.
Lisa has 5 bows.
How many bows
do they have?

Sam has 6 fish.
Mike has 2 fish.
How many fish do
they have in all?

Griffin has 3 bal-
loons. Mike has 8
balloons. How many
balloons do they
have in all?

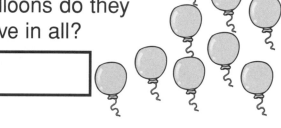

Study and spell the words in this word list.

brave	glad	stone	fast	crop	lost
slip	slap	last	step	stop	list

Unscramble the words. (Clue: You will find them in your word list.)

psla _____   etsno _____   stal _____

ptos _____   rebav _____   solt _____

porc _____   lgda _____   atsf _____

psil _____   epst _____   stil _____

Read each paragraph and circle the sentence that explains the main idea of the paragraph.

1. Emily's umbrella is old. It has holes in it. The color is faded. It doesn't keep the rain off her.

2. Tabby is a tan and white cat. He has a long, white tail. He lives on a farm in the country. Tabby helps the farmer by catching mice in the barn. He sleeps on soft, green hay.

3. There are big, black clouds in the sky. The wind is blowing and it is getting cold. It is going to snow.

Find the opposites in the word search box.

1. The opposite of clean is _____.
2. The opposite of night is _____.
3. The opposite of hot is _____.
4. The opposite of light is _____.
5. The opposite of laugh is _____.
6. The opposite of up is _____.

v	d	i	r	t	y	e	h	k
a	b	a	m	c	e	u	d	g
x	c	r	y	o	d	s	a	j
w	l	h	o	l	r	j	y	n
q	a	z	c	d	d	o	w	n
d	a	r	k	b	s	s	l	m
h	r	e	p	s	t	d	j	p

Subtraction. Draw a line between the pairs that have the same answer.

EXAMPLE:

a. 5 - 3 ——— 6 - 4
    3 - 3   9 - 1

b. 8 - 7   9 - 4
    3 - 1   5 - 3

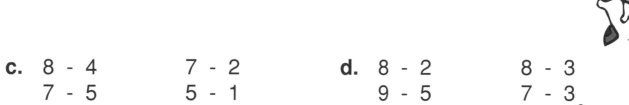

c. 8 - 4   7 - 2
    7 - 5   5 - 1

d. 8 - 2   8 - 3
    9 - 5   7 - 3

e. 10 - 5   7 - 1
   12 - 6   9 - 4
    2 - 0   6 - 0

f. 5 - 5   14 - 7
   12 - 9   8 - 5
   11 - 4   8 - 8

Something is wrong with one word in each sentence. Find the word and correct it!

1. What may i help with?

2. Gve him a brush.

3. You can sti on the chair.

4. Will you miks the paint?

5. Ded you get the pen?

Circle the words that do not belong in the numbered lists below.

EXAMPLE

1. beans	carrots	corn	(balls)	peas	(books)
2. train	boat	leg	car	dress	jet
3. cat	orange	green	blue	red	five
4. lake	ocean	pond	chair	river	shoe
5. bear	apple	lion	wolf	pillow	tiger
6. head	sleep	jump	hop	run	skip
7. Jane	Kathy	Tom	Fred	Jill	Anne
8. park	scared	happy	sad	mad	bee
9. tulip	daffodil	wagon	daisy	basket	rose
10. shirt	socks	bus	rope	pants	dress

Write a story that begins, "My favorite kind of fruit is _____, because..."

_____

- -

_____

_____

- -

_____

_____

- -

_____

_____

- -

_____

_____

- -

_____

Help the dogs find their doggy snacks by drawing a line to match each dog with the correct answer bone.

Circle the letters that spell the ending sounds.

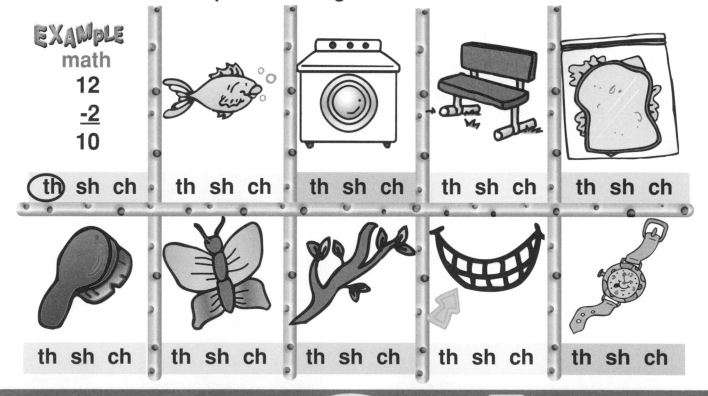

EXAMPLE
math
12
-2
10

(th) sh ch | th sh ch | th sh ch | th sh ch | th sh ch

th sh ch | th sh ch | th sh ch | th sh ch | th sh ch

Fill in the missing (oi) or (oy), then write the word.

b ___ ___

_____

s ___ ___ l

_____

___ ___ ster

_____

t ___ ___

_____

p ___ ___ nt

_____

Write the correct word in the blank.

1. Griffin _____ a song.   **sing**   **sang**

2. Did the bell _____ yet?   **ring**   **rang**

3. The bee _____ the king.   **stung**   **sting**

4. The waves will _____ the ship.   **sank**   **sink**

5. Mom will take a _____ trip.   **ship**   **short**

6. I _____ visit Grandma at home.   **shack**   **shall**

7. Lisa has a _____ on her back.   **rash**   **rush**

8. Trevor likes to _____ in the   **last**   **splash**
   puddles.

Finish the chart.

1. O—|—O—|—O—|—O—|—O—|—O—|
   2   4   6   ____ ____ ____

2. O—|—O—|—O—|—O—|—O—|—O—|
   3 ____ 9 ____ ____ ____

3. O—|—O—|—O—|—O—|—O—|—O—|
   4 ____ 12 ____ ____ ____

2. O—|—O—|—O—|—O—|—O—|—O—|
   5 ____ 15 ____ ____ 30

Use the Word Study List to do the following activity.

Word Study List

go
me
we
he
no
so
she
be
see
bee

1. Write the word "go." Change the beginning letter to make two more words.

    _____ _____ _____

    _____ _____ _____

2. Write the words that mean the opposite of "yes" and "stop."

    _____ _____

    _____ _____

3. Write "she," then write two more words that end the same.

    _____ _____ _____

    _____ _____ _____

Fill in the blank with a homonym for the underlined word. Remember, homonyms sound the same but have different meanings.

made	new	~~eight~~	sea	through
wood	right	bee	hear	knot

EXAMPLE

1. Ashley <u>ate</u> ____eight____ pancakes for breakfast.
2. Stay <u>here</u> and you can _____ the music.
3. Can you <u>see</u> the _____ from the top of the hill?
4. <u>Be</u> careful when you catch a _____.
5. <u>Would</u> you get some _____ for the fire?
6. Did you <u>write</u> the _____ answer?
7. He <u>threw</u> the ball _____ the window.
8. Our <u>maid</u> _____ all the beds.
9. The little girl could <u>not</u> tie a _____ in the rope.
10. My mother <u>knew</u> the _____ teacher.

What did you do yesterday? Write down your activities in the order you did them.

1. _____

2. _____

3. _____

4. _____

5. _____

6. _____

Read and solve the math problem below.

On July 4th, Todd and his friends went to the parade. It was a hot day. Todd bought five snow cones. He gave one to Griffin, one to Ashley, and one to Emily. How many snow cones did Todd have left?

Divide the following compound words. EXAMPLE snow/ball.

1. goldfish

2. blueberry

3. hairbrush

4. yourself

5. railroad

6. sometime

7. daytime

8. grapefruit

9. bedtime

10. popcorn

11. sailboat

12. today

13. spaceship

14. raindrop

15. newspaper

16. doghouse

17. cupcake

18. sidewalk

Read, and answer the questions.

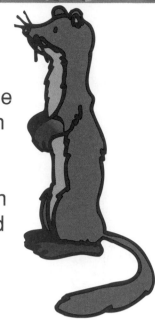

Years ago, many black-footed ferrets lived in the West. They were wild and free. Their habitat was in the flat grasslands. Their habitat was destroyed by man.

The ferrets began to vanish. Almost all of them died. Scientists worked to save the ferrets' lives and now their numbers have increased.

1. Where did the black-footed ferrets live?

_____

2. Who worked to save the ferrets' lives?

_____

3. What happened when the scientists started to work?

_____

How many words can you make using the letters in "camping trip?"

paint

_____

_____

_____

_____

_____

_____

Subtraction.

10	10	10	10	10	10	10	10	10
- 2	- 9	- 7	- 1	- 8	- 3	- 4	- 6	- 5

11	11	11	11	11	11	11	11	11
- 2	- 9	- 7	- 1	- 8	- 3	- 5	- 0	- 6

12	12	12	12	12	12	12	12	12
- 2	- 9	- 7	- 1	- 8	- 3	- 5	- 0	- 6

Write a story.

If I were a firecracker, I would...

_____

_____

_____

_____

_____

_____

_____

_____

Number the sentences in their correct order.

_____ Lisa's friend made a wish and blew out the candles.

_____ Lisa put sixteen blue candles on the cake.

_____ Lisa made a chocolate cake for her friend.

_____ Lisa went to the store and bought a cake mix.

_____ Lisa lit the candles with a match.

Draw a picture of the birthday cake Lisa made for her friend.

Match the sign shapes to the correct answer and then color the signs.

yield
yellow

hospital
blue

railroad crossing
black/white

phone
blue

stop
red

handicapped
blue

Which balloon has the number described by the tens and ones?
Color that balloon. Use the color that is written in each box.

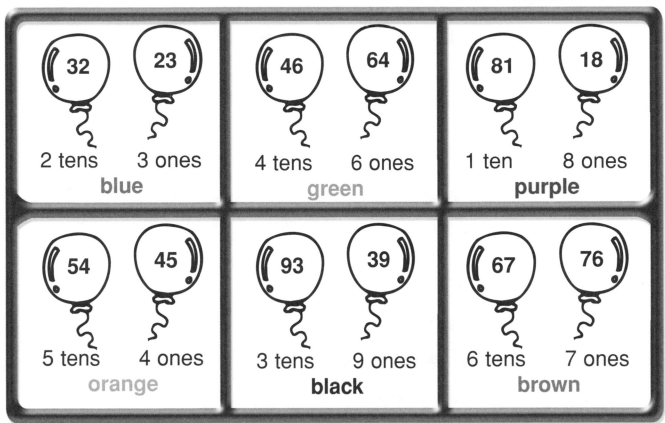

32 23	46 64	81 18
2 tens 3 ones	4 tens 6 ones	1 ten 8 ones
blue	**green**	**purple**
54 45	93 39	67 76
5 tens 4 ones	3 tens 9 ones	6 tens 7 ones
orange	**black**	**brown**

One word is spelled wrong in each sentence. Write the correct word from the word list.

Word Study and Spelling List

help

met

next

leg

pet

net

wet

1. A cat is a good pat. ─ ─ ─ ─ ─ ─ ─ ─ ─ ─ ─ ─ ─ ─ ─ ─ ─

2. She ran to get hlp. ─ ─ ─ ─ ─ ─ ─ ─ ─ ─ ─ ─ ─ ─ ─ ─ ─

3. He sat nekst to her. ─ ─ ─ ─ ─ ─ ─ ─ ─ ─ ─ ─ ─ ─ ─

4. We mit on the bus. ─ ─ ─ ─ ─ ─ ─ ─ ─ ─ ─ ─ ─ ─ ─ ─

5. The dog cut his lag. ─ ─ ─ ─ ─ ─ ─ ─ ─ ─ ─ ─ ─ ─ ─

6. The duck got wit. ─ ─ ─ ─ ─ ─ ─ ─ ─ ─ ─ ─ ─ ─ ─ ─

7. The fish is in the nut. ─ ─ ─ ─ ─ ─ ─ ─ ─ ─ ─ ─ ─ ─

Read the sentences. Circle the nouns (naming words).

EXAMPLE

1. The (horse) lost one of his (shoes)
2. The dog ran after the mailman.
3. A submarine is a kind of boat.
4. The nurse read a book to the sick lady.
5. What kind of sandwich did you have in your lunch?
6. Our teacher showed us a movie about butterflies.
7. The artist drew a beautiful picture of the city.
8. My little sister has a cute teddy bear.
9. Does Mr. Slade have the key for the back door?
10. The boys and girls left for school.

Write the months of the year in the correct order.

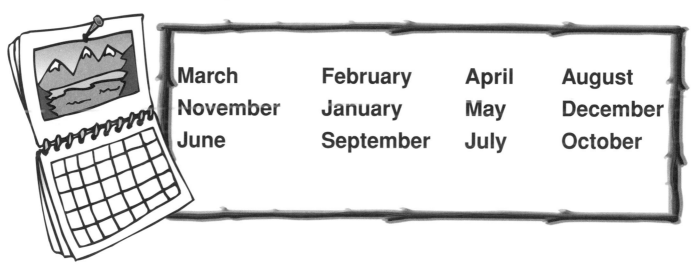

March	February	April	August
November	January	May	December
June	September	July	October

1. _____   7. _____
2. _____   8. _____
3. _____   9. _____
4. _____   10. _____
5. _____   11. _____
6. _____   12. _____

1. Circle the odd numbers in each row.

    a. 2   5   7   3   9   4   6   11

    b. 1   10   6   8   12   13   15   2

    c. 5   11   9   13   14   17   19   3

2. Circle the even numbers in each row.

    a. 6   9   2   11   4   7   3   8

    b. 13   8   10   6   12   16   9   5

    c. 14   16   9   11   12   18   7   4

3. Circle the largest number in each set.

    a. 26 or 32   **c.** 51 or 49   **e.** 41 or 14

    b. 19 or 21   **d.** 80 or 60   **f.** 67 or 76

Write the middle consonant of each word below.

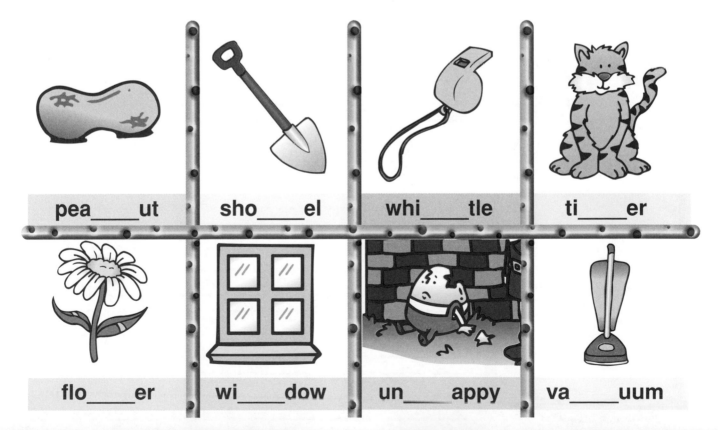

pea____ut   sho____el   whi____tle   ti____er

flo____er   wi____dow   un____appy   va____uum

Read each sentence. Write the correct word on the line.

aw	**au**
hawk	auto

oi	**oy**
oil	boy

1. A dime is a _____.

   coin   point   lawn

2. I want to buy my friend a new _____.

   boy   toy   claw

3. My cat has one white _____.

   paw   saw   car

4. Don has two sons and one _____.

   paw   daughter   boil

Invent, design, and describe a new kind of soda pop!

_____
- - - - - - - - - - - - - - - - - - -
_____
_____
- - - - - - - - - - - - - - - - - - -
_____
_____
- - - - - - - - - - - - - - - - - - -
_____
_____
- - - - - - - - - - - - - - - - - - -
_____
_____
- - - - - - - - - - - - - - - - - - -
_____

Fill in the blank space with a number to get the answer in the box.

4 - _____ =	**3**
3 + _____ =	
2 + _____ =	

5 + _____ =	**6**
2 + _____ =	
9 - _____ =	

7 + _____ =	**8**
_____ - 1 =	
_____ + 2 =	

_____ - 4 =	**5**
8 - _____ =	
3 + _____ =	

Fill in each blank with the correct contraction.

EXAMPLE:

1. cannot _____can't_____

2. I am _____

3. you are _____

4. do not _____

5. he is _____

6. I will _____

7. you have _____

Write the two words that make up the contraction.

8. isn't _____

9. you've _____

10. she's _____

11. couldn't _____

12. we're _____

13. didn't _____

14. they'll _____

Fill in the blanks using <u>is</u> or <u>are</u>. On line 9, write a sentence using <u>is</u>. On line 10, write a sentence using <u>are</u>.

1. We _____ going to town tomorrow.
2. The cows _____ in the field.
3. This book _____ not mine.
4. Where _____ a box of chalk?
5. Seals _____ fast swimmers.
6. _____ he going to help you?
7. It _____ very hot outside today.
8. _____ you going to the circus?
9. _____
10. _____

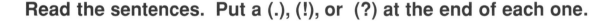

Read the sentences. Put a (.), (!), or (?) at the end of each one.

1. What time do you go to bed____
2. Why did the baby cry____
3. That girl over there is my sister____
4. We do not have our work done____
5. Get out of the way____
6. Are you and I going to the movie____
7. Go shut the door____
8. Do monsters have horns on their heads____
9. My parents are going on a long trip____
10. Look out____ That car will run over you____

Words to Sound, Read, and Spell

Magic e

can	cane
mad	made
cap	cape
man	mane
tap	tape
past	paste
bit	bite
kit	kite
quit	quite
win	wine
rip	ripe
hid	hide
grip	gripe
slid	slide

Long ā words to know!

bake	brake	cave	rake
pale	shape	wake	blaze
state	chase	tape	rate
shade	brave	waste	plane
name	plate	wave	taste
make	made	flake	gave
scale	game	drape	snake
late	lake	vase	scrape
mane	whale	came	base
frame	date	cake	shave
shake	cane	sale	awake
cape	blame	skate	grape
paste	take	trade	
save	glaze	same	

Long ī words

dive	pride	pipe	hide
bite	wipe	while	chime
time	spike	slide	tribe
tire	pie	like	shine
line	tie	die	smile
live	dime	glide	wide
quite	hire	gripe	trike
crime	hive	size	alike
wife	white	prize	stripe
pine	slime	mine	strike
pile	life	five	lie
side	nine	kite	inside
hike	mile	lime	swipe
alive	ride	wire	
ripe	bike	fine	
file	bribe	drive	

Long ō words

rope	wore	hose	home
more	rose	those	
slope	chore	toe	
store	stole	code	
pose	smoke	tone	
quote	bone	drove	
doze	wove	throne	
rode	zone	pole	
stone	stove	mole	
dove	cone	joke	
shone	poke	shore	
hole	froze	note	
chose	hope	those	
hoe	sore	sole	
tore	nose	swore	
scope	score	woke	

ŌK, I know I can do it!

bow	slow	mellow
low	elbow	blow
mow	fellow	
grow	yellow	
snow	willow	
show	pillow	
throw	hallow	
bowl	flow	
own	tomorrow	
grown	rainbow	
thrown	snowman	
flown	window	
blown	widow	

These words say ō, too!

no
so
go
hello
Jell-O
Eskimo
hippo
lingo
jumbo
lasso
banjo
condo

ow and ou

ow

cow	crowd	growl
down	power	prowl
town	shower	chow
gown	towel	brow
clown	now	allow
crown	how	powder
drown	plow	drowsy
frown	owl	chowder
brown	howl	

ouch

out	found	mouse
shout	round	sour
about	sound	flour
trout	pound	ground
scout	count	account
loud	mount	thousand
cloud	around	discount
aloud	surround	county
bound	house	

oi words

oil	join
boil	joint
coil	point
soil	appoint
broil	disappoin
spoil	poison
void	
coin	

au words
haul
fault
vault
fraud
cause
haunt
haunted
launch
gauze
because

oy words
boy
toy
joy
enjoy
joyful
loyal
royal
cowboy
tomboy
corduroy
convoy
employ
soybean

aw words
dawn
fawn
drawn
claw
straw
lawyer
hawk
crawl
shawl
awful
seesaw
outlaw

ai says ā
pain	rain	quail
main	saint	grain
paint	maid	faith
paid	pail	strain
jail	brain	snail
stain	wait	
bait	afraid	
braid	nail	
sail	plain	
train	laid	
trail	tail	
aid	chain	
mail	faint	
fail	raid	

Two e's are better than one!

see	keep	cheese	nineteen	beep	squeeze
deep	geese	meet	tree	street	need
seem	beet	fifteen	sneeze	creep	peel
sweet	three	Jeep	peek	sheep	wheel
weep	breeze	sleet	feed	screech	
sheet	seek	sleep	cheek	bleed	
sweep	seed	reef	weed	deed	
speech	feel	seen	teen	bee	
green	tweed	steel	screen	peep	
queen	speed	beef	sixteen	freeze	
teeth	greed	feet	wee	free	

Soft c: ce, ci, cy

cent	mice	office
celery	spice	fancy
center	race	mercy
cereal	fence	spicy
cement	nice	lacy
celebrate	circus	officer
ice	circle	medicine
dance	pencil	face
once	excited	place
twice	decide	
slice	exciting	
space	recipe	

ea says ē

sea	beast	cream	peak	clean
leave	seat	eat	lead	feast
meal	leader	reach	leap	neat
dream	leak	bean	deal	beaver
flea	bead	east	team	beak
peach	treat	meat	pea	read
real	reason	beach	weave	cheat
scream	seam	lean	steal	season
heat	tea	yeast	steam	weak
preach	heave	wheat	beat	grease
mean	seal	teacher	teach	

Map Your Course

Make a treasure map for your yard or neighborhood. Decorate a shoe box like a treasure chest and fill it with a treat or special note. Hide it and have your friends follow your map until they find their treasure!

Crossword Puzzle

Choose a topic like sports, geography or music and create your own crossword puzzle. List clues for each word across and down; don't forget to number them. Challenge your friends and family to figure it out.

Try Something New

Fun Activity Ideas

 1 Play hopscotch, marbles, or jump rope.

 2 Visit a fire station.

 3 Take a walk around your neighborhood. Name all of the trees and flowers you can.

 4 Make up a song.

 5 Make a hut out of blankets and chairs.

 6 Put a note in a helium balloon and let it go.

 7 Start a journal. Write about your favorite vacation memories.

 8 Make 3-D nature art. Glue leaves, twigs, dirt, grass, and rocks on paper.

 9 Find an ant colony. Spill some food and see what happens.

 10 Play charades.

 11 Make up a story by drawing pictures.

 12 Do something to help the environment. Clean up an area near your house.

 13 Weed a row in the garden. Mom will love it!

 14 Take a trip to a park.

 15 Learn about different road signs.

Subtraction.

A.

15	14	16	17	13
- 4	- 2	- 8	- 3	- 4

B.

10	18	13	11	16
- 4	- 7	- 6	- 9	- 5

C.

17	12	10	18	19
- 8	- 5	- 1	- 4	- 9

Synonyms are words that have the same or nearly the same meaning. Find a synonym in the word bank for each of the words below. Write the word in the blank space.

happy   big   ill   start

easy   close   scared   large

tidy   copy   quick   funny

begin	_____	afraid	_____	trace	_____
sick	_____	shut	_____	fast	_____
glad	_____	simple	_____	silly	_____
large	_____	big	_____	neat	_____

Unscramble the scrambled word in each sentence and write it correctly.

1. A <u>brzea</u> is an animal in the zoo. _____

2. The robin has <u>nowlf</u> away. _____

3. We mixed flour and eggs in a <u>owlb</u>. _____

4. Button your button and zip your <u>rpzipe</u>. _____

5. A lot of <u>leppeo</u> were at the game. _____

6. We met our new teacher <u>yatdo</u>. _____

7. My old <u>oessh</u> do not fit my feet. _____

8. We made a list of <u>ngtihs</u> to get. _____

9. Jim got <u>irtyd</u> when he fell in the mud. _____

10. <u>eSktri</u> three and you're out. _____

Draw a monster and label the following parts:

stomach, forehead, tongue, throat, feet, arms, eyes, mouth, legs, nose, and any other parts not listed.

Addition.

```
  3      6      9      5      4      2      3      5
  5      4      2      1      3      3      3      5
+ 2    + 3    + 2    + 2    + 4    + 5    + 4    + 3
```

```
  4      7      1      6      2      8      4      3
  5      2      8      1      3      2      2      7
+ 3    + 1    + 1    + 4    + 2    + 3    + 6    + 1
```

7 + 3 + 1 = _____   8 + 2 + 2 = _____   3 + 5 + 1 = _____

Read the sentences. Find a synonym for each underlined word. Write the new word on the lines. A synonym is a word that has the same or nearly the same meaning as another.

automobile	small	glad	rush

The baby is very <u>tiny</u>.

_____
- - - - - - - - - - - - - -
_____

The <u>car</u> ran out of gas.

_____
- - - - - - - - - - - - - -
_____

Susan won, so she was very <u>happy</u>.

_____
- - - - - - - - - - - - - -
_____

My mother was in a big <u>hurry</u>.

_____
- - - - - - - - - - - - - -
_____

COOKIE JAR PUBLISHING

Make an (X) by the answers to the questions.

How is a snake like a turtle?

_____ 1. They both have shells.

_____ 2. They both can be found on land.

_____ 3. They are both reptiles.

_____ 4. They both fly in the sky.

_____ 5. They both have tails.

_____ 6. They both eat flies.

_____ 7. They both have legs.

How is a bike like a truck?

_____ 1. They both have tires.

_____ 2. They both need gas.

_____ 3. They both can be different colors.

_____ 4. They can both be new and shiny.

_____ 5. They both have four wheels.

_____ 6. They both can go.

_____ 7. You can ride in both of them.

How is a sailor like a doctor?

_____ 1. They both wear white.

_____ 2. They both wear hats.

_____ 3. They both work with dogs.

_____ 4. They both are people.

_____ 5. Their job is to help sick people.

_____ 6. They have to work on a ship.

_____ 7. They both should be helpful.

Finish the story.

One day Ashley went out to play. Her friend, Lisa, was already outside.

Lisa said to Ashley, "Let's go play…"

Color in the correct fraction of each picture.

EXAMPLE:

$\frac{1}{2}$ $\frac{1}{3}$ $\frac{1}{4}$

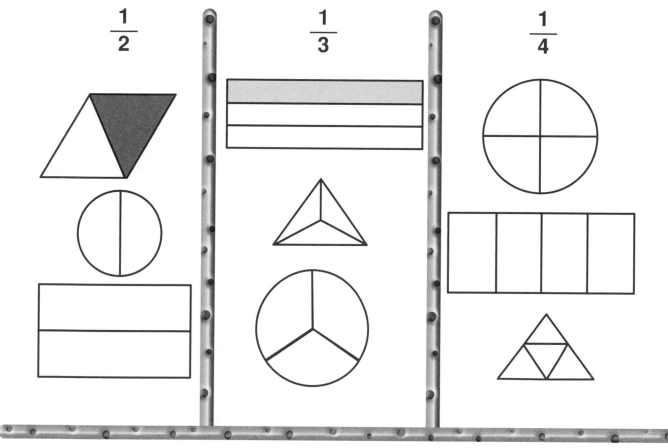

Color the matching bat and ball with the same color.

EXAMPLE

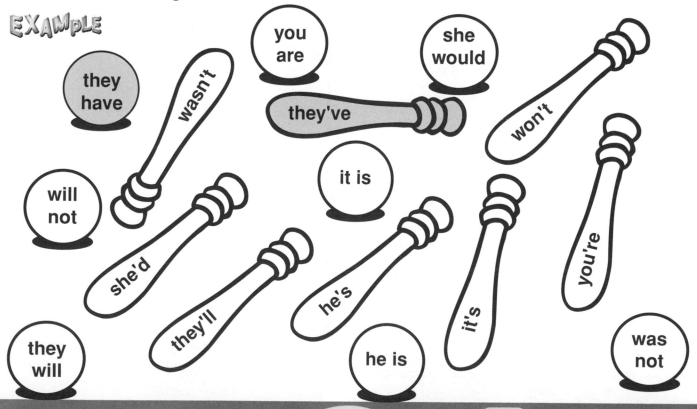

COOKIE JAR PUBLISHING

Make up five funny sentences using one word from each column on the hot-air balloon. Do not use any of the words more than once.

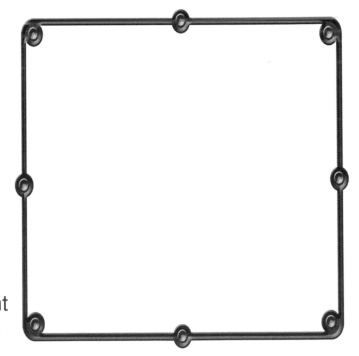

children   held
robbers   fed
bugs   followed
bears   found
birds   dropped

1. _____ the balloons.

2. _____ a big truck.

3. _____ the silly cow.

4. _____ the green frog.

5. _____ all the people.

Read the words in the right column. Write the words in alphabetical order in the left column. Draw your favorite animal in the box.

1. _____ pig

2. _____ horse

3. _____ cat

4. _____ frog

5. _____ ant

6. _____ bear

7. _____ giraffe

8. _____ deer

9. _____ elephant

10. _____ monkey

Add or subtract.

11	18	3	10	17	13	18	19
+7	+1	+7	-3	-2	+6	-6	-7

33	64	5	2	12	14	27	16
+5	-3	+3	+4	-7	-11	-3	-8

17 + 2 = _____   11 - 3 = _____   13 + 5 = _____

Unscramble the words.

psto _____   ithkn _____

sfat _____   oonn _____

ltpae _____   ppayh _____

pste _____   seay _____

gbrni _____   dbyo _____

rdnki _____   stfri _____

enwt _____   yrc _____

Read the words aloud, then write them in alphabetical order.

rabbit

snake

lion

dog

fish

dish

make

candy

puppy

vase

1. _____

_____

2. _____

_____

3. _____

_____

4. _____

_____

5. _____

_____

6. _____

_____

7. _____

_____

8. _____

_____

9. _____

_____

10. _____

_____

Dairy designs. A dairy company has asked you to create a design for a milk carton. Create and color an original milk carton design for the company.

Color the coins that match the given amount.

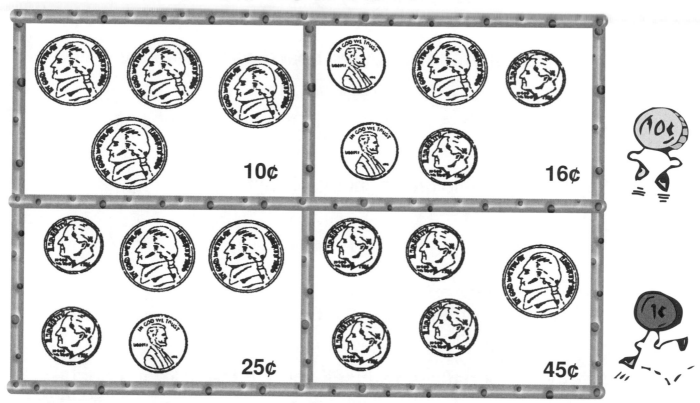

Match the homonyms. Homonyms are words that sound the same but have different meanings.

EXAMPLE

ate	heel	flower	through
cent	sea	threw	pair
knight	night	pain	hear
our	one	pear	flour
write	right	know	pane
knew	sent	here	male
heal	eight	maid	blew
see	hare	mail	no
hair	new	sail	made
won	hour	blue	sale

COOKIE JAR PUBLISHING

Read these silly sentences! Put a by your favorite sentence.

1. You can spend a day at the beach without money.

2. A yardstick has three feet, but it really cannot walk.

3. You might whip cream, but it will not cry.

4. It is not mean to beat scrambled eggs.

5. Rain falls sometimes, but it never gets hurt.

6. You do not eat a whole lot if you eat the hole of a donut.

Draw four things that belong in each box.

Things in the sky.

Things in the ocean.

Things in a cave.

Add or subtract.

1.
$$\begin{array}{r} 10 \\ -\ 4 \\ \hline \end{array} \quad \begin{array}{r} 18 \\ -14 \\ \hline \end{array} \quad \begin{array}{r} 7 \\ -\ 3 \\ \hline \end{array} \quad \begin{array}{r} 7 \\ +\ 5 \\ \hline \end{array} \quad \begin{array}{r} 8 \\ +\ 2 \\ \hline \end{array} \quad \begin{array}{r} 6 \\ -\ 4 \\ \hline \end{array} \quad \begin{array}{r} 9 \\ -\ 4 \\ \hline \end{array} \quad \begin{array}{r} 4 \\ +\ 7 \\ \hline \end{array} \quad \begin{array}{r} 9 \\ +2 \\ \hline \end{array}$$

2.
$$\begin{array}{r} 11 \\ -\ 1 \\ \hline \end{array} \quad \begin{array}{r} 11 \\ +\ 8 \\ \hline \end{array} \quad \begin{array}{r} 10 \\ -\ 8 \\ \hline \end{array} \quad \begin{array}{r} 9 \\ +\ 8 \\ \hline \end{array} \quad \begin{array}{r} 8 \\ +\ 2 \\ \hline \end{array} \quad \begin{array}{r} 9 \\ +\ 1 \\ \hline \end{array} \quad \begin{array}{r} 7 \\ -\ 5 \\ \hline \end{array} \quad \begin{array}{r} 10 \\ -\ 3 \\ \hline \end{array} \quad \begin{array}{r} 11 \\ -\ 7 \\ \hline \end{array}$$

$8 + 6 =$ _____ $9 + 3 =$ _____ $4 + 9 =$ _____

Antonyms. Match the words with opposite meanings.

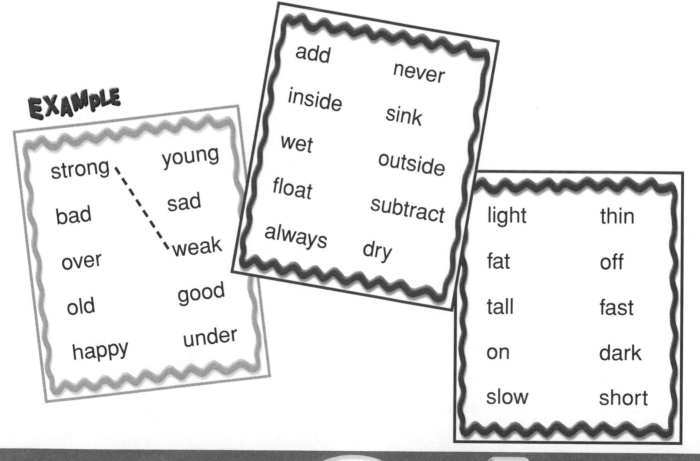

EXAMPLE

strong — young
bad — sad
over — weak
old — good
happy — under

add — never
inside — sink
wet — outside
float — subtract
always — dry

light — thin
fat — off
tall — fast
on — dark
slow — short

Read each sentence. Do what it tells you to do. Then put a ✔ in the box to show that you have finished it.

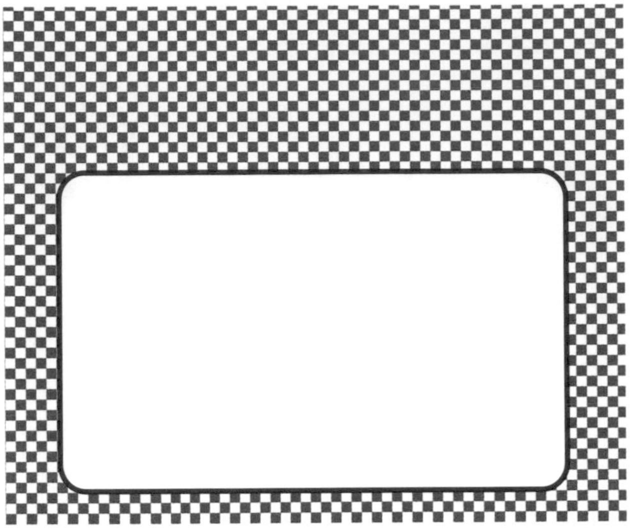

Let's get ready for lunch.

☐ Draw a plate on the placemat.

☐ Draw a napkin on the left side of the plate.

☐ Draw a fork on the napkin.

☐ Draw a knife and spoon on the right side of the plate.

☐ Draw a glass of purple juice above the napkin.

☐ Draw your favorite lunch.

Enjoy!

Writing.

If I could fly anywhere, I would fly to _____
because... _____

_____

_____

_____

_____

_____

_____

_____

_____

_____

Finish each table.

Add 10	
EXAMPLE: 5	15
8	
7	
9	
3	
4	

Add 8	
2	
6	
4	
7	
3	
5	

Add 6	
10	
6	
8	
7	
4	
5	

Circle the correctly spelled word in each row.

1. ca'nt   can'nt   can't
2. esy   easy   eazy
3. crie   cri   cry
4. kea   key   kee
5. buy   buye   biy
6. lihg   light   ligte
7. allready   already   alredy
8. summ   som   some
9. sekond   secund   second
10. hasn't   has'nt   hasent

11. wonce   onse   once
12. pritty   preety   pretty
13. carry   carey   carrie
14. you're   yure   yo're
15. parte   part   parrt
16. star   stor   starr
17. funy   funny   funnie
18. babie   babey   baby
19. mabe   maybe   maybee
20. therde   therd   third

Circle the correct answer.

1. Another name for boy is: girl   son   funny
2. After seven comes: six   nine   eight
3. I bite with: wheel   teeth   arms
4. A car and truck roll on: with   whip   wheels
5. A farmer grows: ship   wheat   land
6. Your brain helps you: this   thing   think
7. A chair can also be a: seat   sound   safe
8. A rabbit has: while   whirl   whiskers

Do the crossword puzzle.

Word List

cent

sent

here

night

write

weight

Down

1. A penny is worth one _____.

2. My friend _____ me a letter.

3. Please _____ your name.

Across

1. Will you please come _____?

2. When the sun goes down, it is _____.

3. The doctor checked my _____.

Make number sentences. Remember: Use only the numbers in the circles.

EXAMPLE:

(Circle) 13 8 5

(Circle) 12 5 7

__8__ + __5__ = __13__
____ + ____ = ____
____ - ____ = ____
____ - ____ = ____

____ + ____ = ____
____ + ____ = ____
____ - ____ = ____
____ - ____ = ____

(Circle) 14 8 6

(Circle) 6 9 15

____ + ____ = ____
____ + ____ = ____
____ - ____ = ____
____ - ____ = ____

____ + ____ = ____
____ + ____ = ____
____ - ____ = ____
____ - ____ = ____

Put the words under the correct sound-picture.

Word List

bone	fox
those	coat
log	rock
drove	top
job	rope
note	dock

long (ō) nose   short (ŏ) pop

1. _____
2. _____
3. _____
4. _____
5. _____
6. _____

1. _____
2. _____
3. _____
4. _____
5. _____
6. _____

Read the sentences. Circle and write the action verb in each sentence.

EXAMPLE

1. The chicken (ran) away. _____ran_____
2. Judy cut her finger with the knife. _____
3. A kangaroo can hop very fast. _____
4. I like to swim in our pool. _____
5. Ted and Sid will chop some wood. _____
6. That kitten likes to climb trees. _____
7. We will eat dinner at six o'clock. _____
8. The baby was yawning. _____
9. The car crashed into a tree. _____
10. Please peel this orange for me. _____

Draw a face beside each statement that tells how it makes you feel.

1. a rainy day

2. chocolate cake

3. playing soccer

4. camping in the mountains

5. fighting with a friend

6. taking a bath

7. birthday presents

8. eating beans and corn

9. catching a fly ball

10. going to Grandmother's

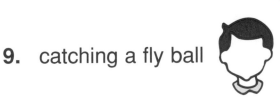

Add.

1.
$$\begin{array}{r} 3 \\ 2 \\ +1 \\ \hline \end{array} \quad \begin{array}{r} 3 \\ 4 \\ +2 \\ \hline \end{array} \quad \begin{array}{r} 6 \\ 1 \\ +2 \\ \hline \end{array} \quad \begin{array}{r} 2 \\ 2 \\ +3 \\ \hline \end{array} \quad \begin{array}{r} 4 \\ 3 \\ +3 \\ \hline \end{array} \quad \begin{array}{r} 5 \\ 4 \\ +6 \\ \hline \end{array} \quad \begin{array}{r} 7 \\ 1 \\ +2 \\ \hline \end{array} \quad \begin{array}{r} 3 \\ 5 \\ +4 \\ \hline \end{array}$$

2.
$$\begin{array}{r} 1 \\ 3 \\ +2 \\ \hline \end{array} \quad \begin{array}{r} 6 \\ 3 \\ +1 \\ \hline \end{array} \quad \begin{array}{r} 7 \\ 2 \\ +1 \\ \hline \end{array} \quad \begin{array}{r} 4 \\ 5 \\ +2 \\ \hline \end{array} \quad \begin{array}{r} 5 \\ 2 \\ +3 \\ \hline \end{array} \quad \begin{array}{r} 4 \\ 4 \\ +1 \\ \hline \end{array} \quad \begin{array}{r} 8 \\ 1 \\ +2 \\ \hline \end{array} \quad \begin{array}{r} 4 \\ 6 \\ +3 \\ \hline \end{array}$$

Write soft (c) words under pencil. Write hard (c) words under candy.

| grocery | cattle | cement | corn | price |
| cake | cellar | crib | grace | cow |

pencil    candy

1. _____   1. _____

2. _____   2. _____

3. _____   3. _____

4. _____   4. _____

5. _____   5. _____

Unscramble the sentences. Write the words in the correct order.

1. sun shine will today The.

   ----

2. mile today I a walked.

   ----

3. house We painted our.

   ----

4. Mother knit will I something for.

Write a letter. Ask someone to a silly picnic.

Start your letter with "Dear _____,"
End your letter with "Yours truly, _____."

Color the shape that matches the description.

10 (octagon)
2 tens

23 (diamond)
3 ones

green

17 (triangle)
5 tens

57 (banner)
7 ones

purple

52 (rectangle)
5 tens

59 (circle)
2 ones

yellow

23 (square)
2 tens

32 (octagon)
3 ones

orange

39 (circle)
3 tens

29 (flag)
9 ones

red

10 (circle)
1 ten

20 (banner)
0 ones

blue

Write each word under the correct sound picture.

| tower | blow | mow | clown | elbow | crown |
| flown | bowls | how | frown | own | brown |

cow

pillow

Draw a line to the right word.

EXAMPLE

1. Something near you is   clock
2. Something that tells time is a   bird
3. A time of day is   babies
4. A crow is a kind of   snoop
5. A place where fish live is an   close
6. Pork is a kind of   dusk
7. Chicks, ducklings, and fawns are kinds of   aquarium
8. A shop is a kind of   strike
9. To hit something is to   store
10. To look in someone else's things is to   meat

Write as many words as you can that describe:

ice cream

watermelon

Subtract.

57	68	96	57	38	59	64	77	54
-32	-44	-92	-43	- 3	-45	-42	-34	-20

83	75	48	95	68	39	89	93	69
-62	-20	- 4	-31	-26	-10	-53	-10	-35

19	24	52	63	76	88	90	71	29
- 3	-11	-31	-41	-22	-44	-30	-51	-15

Write in the name of each picture and color.

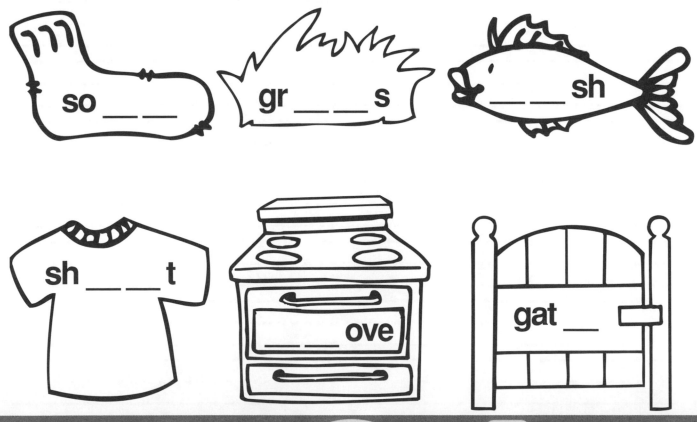

so ____

gr ____ s

____ ____ sh

sh ____ ____ t

____ ____ ove

gat ____

Read each sentence. Do what it tells you to do. Then put a ✔ in the box to show that you have finished it.

Let's go to the park and play.

- ☐ Draw a swingset.
- ☐ Draw a slide.
- ☐ Draw a sandpile.
- ☐ Draw green grass.
- ☐ Draw one apple tree.
- ☐ Draw a yellow sun in the sky.
- ☐ Draw a blue sky.

Have fun!

Before school starts again, I want to...

Finish each table.

EXAMPLE

subtract 5	
9	4
5	
7	
10	
11	
8	

subtract 3	
10	
9	
7	
8	
6	
11	

subtract 2	
11	
7	
9	
5	
8	
6	

Circle the right r-controlled vowel.

EXAMPLE   b(i)rd

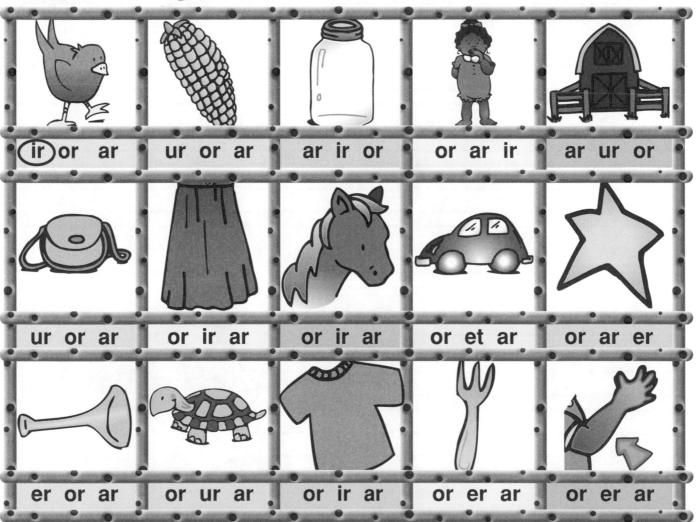

ir or ar   ur or ar   ar ir or   or ar ir   ar ur or

ur or ar   or ir ar   or ir ar   or et ar   or ar er

er or ar   or ur ar   or ir ar   or er ar   or er ar

Complete the riddles.

1. I am rather tiny. I have wings and buzz around. I can be a real pest at picnics. I am a _____.

2. I was just born. My mother and father feed me and keep me dry. I cry, and sleep, but I cannot walk. I am a _____.

3. I am made of metal and am quite little. I can lock things up and open them, too! I am a _____.

4. I like to sing. I lay eggs. I like to eat bugs and worms. I am a _____.

Write a story about spiders.

Math. Below are two mileage maps. Use them to answer the questions.

How many miles from Salt Lake City to Bountiful? _____ miles.

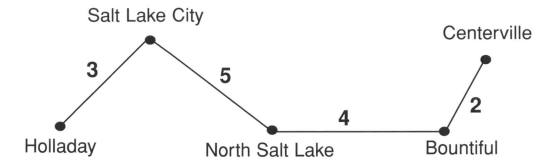

How many miles from Provo to Pleasant Grove? _____ miles.

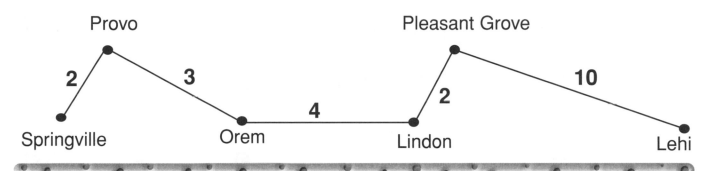

Read the sentences. Is the underlined word in each sentence right or wrong? Circle the correct answer.

1. Jane is a very <u>brav</u> girl.   right   (wrong)
2. The American flag is red, white, and <u>bloo</u>.   right   wrong
3. Those girls are in my <u>class</u>.   right   wrong
4. Mike is a very <u>helpfull</u> friend.   right   wrong
5. I remembered to turn off the <u>light</u>.   right   wrong
6. This candy is sticky <u>stuf</u>.   right   wrong
7. Is <u>shee</u> coming with us?   right   wrong
8. May I <u>yooz</u> your book?   right   wrong
9. Don't <u>lose</u> your boots.   right   wrong
10. Our baby is so <u>cute</u>.   right   wrong

Noisy or quiet? Put an <u>N</u> in front of things that are noisy and a <u>Q</u> in front of things that are quiet. Draw a noisy picture and a quiet picture.

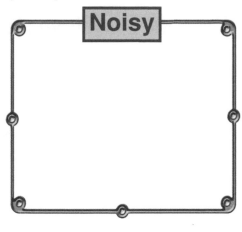

____1.   A butterfly flying through the air.

____2.   A cook using a mixer to make a cake.

____3.   Popcorn popping on the stove.

____4.   A dress hanging up to dry.

____5.   A child reading to herself.

____6.   Ice cream melting in the sun.

____7.   A cat and dog fighting in the driveway.

____8.   A band marching in a parade.

Homonyms. The following words sound the same but have two different meanings. Write two sentences using the different meanings.

bat: a wooden stick that is used to hit a ball
           a small animal that flies at night

_____

_____

_____

spring: the season of the year between winter and summer
              to jump or bounce into the air

_____

_____

_____

Words to Sound, Read, and Spell

ar
car	harm	chart
far	charm	party
jar	barn	bark
star	yarn	dark
scar	art	mark
yard	dart	park
card	cart	shark
hard	part	spark
arm	smart	
farm	start	

or
for	born	dorm
fort	corn	form
sort	worn	torch
short	thorn	porch
sport	north	order
cork	forth	organ
fork	forty	story
pork	horse	history
stork	storm	

er
her
clerk
perch
nerve
verb
fern
were
serve

ir
dirt
shirt
first
third
swirl
skirt
firm
bird
thirst
twirl

ur
hurt
spurt
burnt
burp
curl
turtle
purple
church

Remember these special sounds!

sh
shed	brush
shell	slash
ship	flash
shack	clash
shag	trash
shin	crash
shock	smash
shot	fish
shop	dish
shuck	fresh
wish	
hush	
mush	
rush	

ch
check	inch
chess	pinch
chick	chug
chill	chap
chin	chaff
chip	
chop	
chum	
chat	
much	
such	
rich	
which	

th
this
them
that
thud
math
with
moth
thin
then
thick
bath
path
cloth
path

tch
hatch
patch
stitch
scotch
catch
ditch

wh
when
where
whip
why
what

Compound words surprise us!
pancake	rosebud
cupcake	bluebird
handshake	blueberry
cannot	frostbite
sunset	potpie
suntan	necktie
sandbox	wishbone
swingset	fireman
pineapple	nickname
sunrise	drumstick
sunshine	checkup
underline	
tiptoe	
bathrobe	

Here are -nt, -nd, -nk, and -ng words.

-nt
ant	spent
pant	mint
plant	hint
bent	print
dent	flint
rent	hunt
sent	stunt
tent	punt
vent	runt
went	

-nd
and	blond
band	end
hand	bend
sand	send
land	lend
stand	tend
grand	spend
bond	wind
pond	fund

-nk
bank	wink
yank	blink
sank	drink
tank	stink
drank	think
crank	honk
spank	bunk
ink	junk
pink	drunk
sink	skunk

-ng
bang	long
rang	strong
hang	king
hung	sing
sung	wing
stung	bring
flung	swing
swung	thing
gong	

What about -y at the end of words?
any	penny
many	puppy
very	sloppy
messy	happy
sticky	cherry
windy	angry
sandy	hungry
handy	sixty
copy	fifty
body	day
daddy	say
muddy	clay
candy	sway
twenty	may
dizzy	way
yummy	stay
funny	away
sunny	

These, too, are interesting!
key	donkey	monkey	turkey
keys	donkeys	monkeys	turkeys

These are interesting words!

be	fume	dude
me	amuse	duke
he	abuse	tune
we	accuse	tube
she	value	few
eve	rescue	new
theme	continue	grew
extreme	blue	knew
complete	true	threw
compete	clue	crew
athlete	glue	drew
these	flute	news
cue	fluke	jewel
cute	rude	blew
cube	rule	flew
mule	prune	nephew
mute	due	stew
fuse	dune	

Here are some more -y words!

cry	flying
why	crying
shy	trying
fry	typing
try	rhyming
by	hockey
fly	jockey
my	alley
sky	valley
spy	nosy
bye	trolley
lye	money
type	chimney
style	honey
rhyme	parsley

What about these?

fly	flies
try	tries
cry	tried
fry	cries
	cried
	fries
	fried

Let's add the -s and -es sound.

flags	boxes	stitches
plants	foxes	crutches
hands	axes	matches
pets	sixes	benches
steps	buzzes	inches
belts	quizzes	patches
kids	buses	hatches
gifts	glasses	catches
bricks	kisses	pitches
dogs	dresses	stitches
socks	classes	blotches
songs	wishes	sketches
bugs	brushes	switches
trucks	dishes	
ducks	branches	

These words end with -ing.

jumping	coasting	whizzing
planting	peeking	winning
thinking	feeling	shopping
yelling	screaming	hugging
singing	reaching	tugging
catching	sailing	running
fishing	reading	swimming
quacking	making	hitting
poking	hoping	hopping
shaking	shining	sitting
riding	hiding	stopping
waving	skating	digging
smiling	diving	petting
joking	saving	grinning
floating	sledding	wagging

Add -ed and what do you get?

added	tested	grinned
ended	dumped	hugged
handed	crossed	dragged
mended	tripped	fanned
hinted	dropped	hummed
acted	snapped	tugged
dented	hopped	joked
dusted	camped	hiked
carted	missed	smiled
started	dripped	stared
rented	stopped	waved
petted	passed	cared
nodded	pumped	choked
rested	farmed	shaped
drifted	harmed	

Let's go for the -le endings.

paddle	sniffle	dimple
saddle	apple	simple
middle	bubble	handle
riddle	gobble	candle
puddle	dribble	tackle
cuddle	pebble	freckle
battle	wiggle	pickle
rattle	jiggle	tickle
kettle	giggle	twinkle
little	juggle	sprinkle
bottle	snuggle	buckle
dazzle	mumble	chuckle
sizzle	tumble	uncle
puzzle	stumble	tangle
raffle	crumble	dangle

Let's read contractions!

are	have	is, has	will	would, had
you're	I've	he's	I'll	I'd
we're	you've	it's	she'll	she'd
they're	we've	she's	he'll	you'd
who're	they've	what's	it'll	who'd
	could've	that's	we'll	he'd
us	should've	who's	they'll	they'd
let's	would've	there's	that'll	
		here's	who'll	
am		one's	you'll	
I'm				

How about these endings?

bigger	camper	children
fatter	winner	chicken
fattest	runner	ladder
fresher	swimmer	matter
freshest	singer	better
sicker	happen	dresser
sickest	fasten	pepper
longer	often	zipper
longest	rotten	dinner
pitcher	gotten	robber
kicker	bitten	offer
hunter	kitten	butter
helper	kitchen	bumper

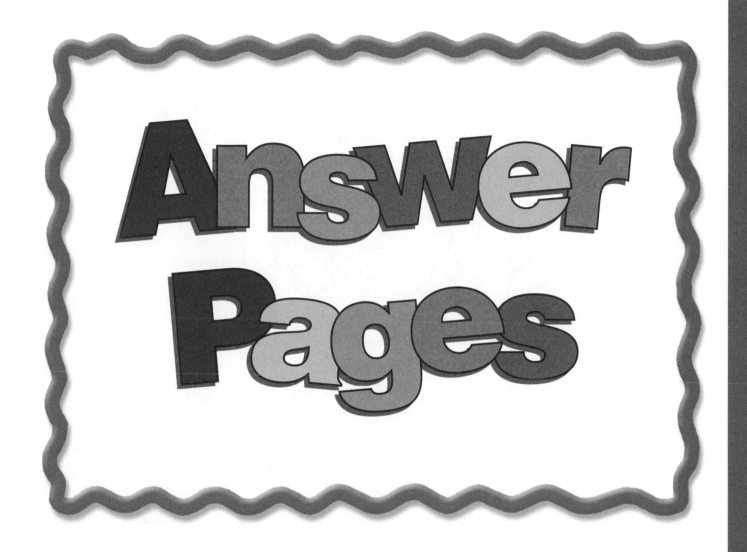

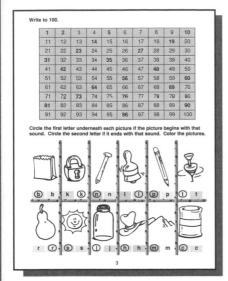

Page 3

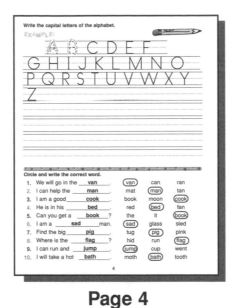

Page 4

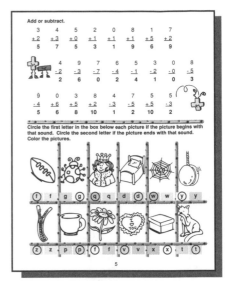

Page 5

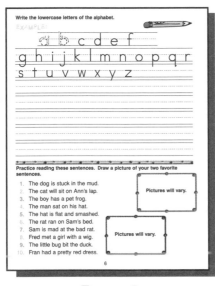

Page 6

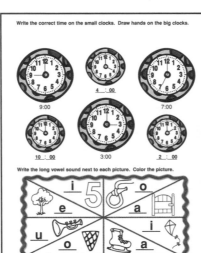

Page 7

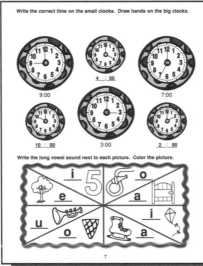

Page 8

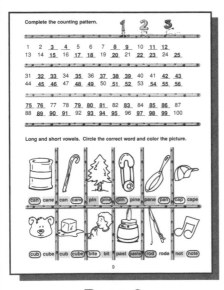

Page 9

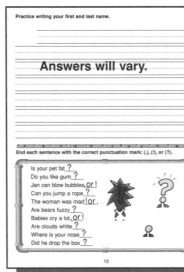

Page 10

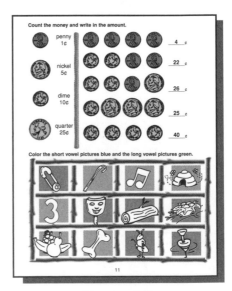

Page 11

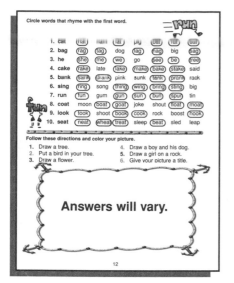

Page 12

Circle words that rhyme with the first word.

1. cat — hat, ham, cat, pig, dim, hut, bat
2. bag — rag, tag, dog, tag, nag, big, sag
3. he — she, me, we, go, see, be, tree
4. cake — rake, late, lake, make, bake, stake, said
5. bank — sank, drank, pink, sunk, tank, prank, rack
6. sing — ring, song, thing, wing, bring, sting, big
7. run — fun, gum, gun, sun, bun, spun, tin
8. coat — moon, boat, goat, joke, shout, float, moat
9. look — took, shoot, book, cook, rock, boost, hook
10. seat — neat, wheat, treat, sleep, beat, sled, leap

Follow these directions and color your picture.

1. Draw a tree.
2. Put a bird in your tree.
3. Draw a flower.
4. Draw a boy and his dog.
5. Draw a girl on a rock.
6. Give your picture a title.

Answers will vary.

12

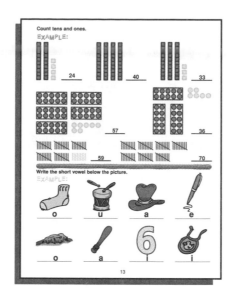

Page 13

Count tens and ones.
EXAMPLE:

24   40   33

57   36

59   70

Write the short vowel below the picture.
EXAMPLE:

o   u   a   e

o   a   i   i

13

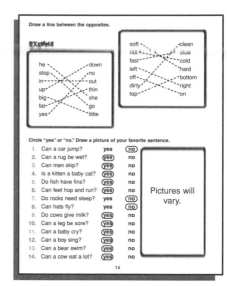

Page 14

Draw a line between the opposites.

EXAMPLE

he — down
stop — no
in — out
up — thin
big — she
fat — go
yes — little

soft — clean
hot — slow
fast — cold
left — hard
off — bottom
dirty — right
top — on

Circle "yes" or "no." Draw a picture of your favorite sentence.

1. Can a car jump? — no
2. Can a rug be wet? — yes
3. Can men skip? — yes
4. Is a kitten a baby cat? — yes
5. Do fish have fins? — yes
6. Can feet hop and run? — yes
7. Do rocks need sleep? — no
8. Can hats fly? — no
9. Do cows give milk? — yes
10. Can a leg be sore? — yes
11. Can a baby cry? — yes
12. Can a boy sing? — yes
13. Can a bear swim? — yes
14. Can a cow eat a lot? — yes

Pictures will vary.

14

Page 15

Read and answer these math problems.

1. Griffin has two green cars and eight red cars in his train. How many cars does Griffin have in all?

__2__ green cars __8__ red cars __10__ cars in train

2. There were five birds in one nest. Then two birds flew away. How many birds were left in the nest?

5 − 2 = 3

3. Matt had nine spelling words. He missed two words. How many words did he get right?

9 − 2 = 7

For each set of words, write the contraction in the word blank.

1. it is — it's
2. you will — you'll
3. I am — I'm
4. we will — we'll
5. they have — they've
6. he will — he'll

we'll   it's   you'll   I'm   he'll   they've

15

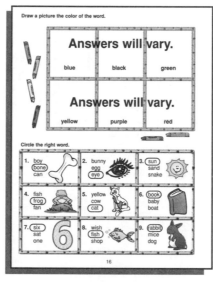

Page 16

Draw a picture the color of the word.

Answers will vary.
blue   black   green

Answers will vary.
yellow   purple   red

Circle the right word.

1. boy, bone, can
2. bunny, egg, eye
3. sun, sand, snake
4. fish, frog, fan
5. yellow, cow, cat
6. book, baby, boat
7. six, sat, one
8. wish, fish, shop
9. rabbit, mice, dog

16

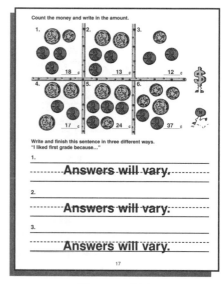

Page 17

Count the money and write in the amount.

1. 18 c   2. 13 c   3. 12 c
4. 17 c   5. 24 c   6. 37 c

Write and finish this sentence in three different ways.
"I liked first grade because..."

1. Answers will vary.

2. Answers will vary.

3. Answers will vary.

17

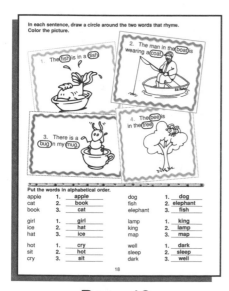

Page 18

In each sentence, draw a circle around the two words that rhyme. Color the picture.

1. The fish is in a dish.
2. The man in the boat is wearing a coat.
3. There is a bug in my mug.
4. The bee is in the tree.

Put the words in alphabetical order.

apple   1. apple
cat   2. book
book   3. cat

girl   1. girl
ice   2. hat
hat   3. ice

hot   1. cry
sit   2. hot
cry   3. sit

dog   1. dog
fish   2. elephant
elephant 3. fish

lamp   1. king
king   2. lamp
map   3. map

well   1. dark
sleep   2. sleep
dark   3. well

18

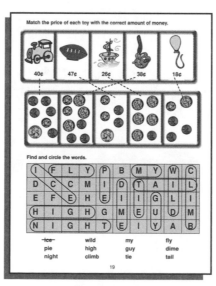

Page 19

Match the price of each toy with the correct amount of money.

40¢   47¢   26¢   38¢   18¢

Find and circle the words.

I	F	L	Y	P	B	M	Y	W	C
D	C	C	M	I	D	T	A	I	L
E	F	E	H	E	I	I	G	L	I
H	I	G	H	G	M	E	U	D	M
N	I	G	H	T	E	I	Y	A	B

ice   wild   my   fly
pie   high   guy   dime
night climb tie   tail

19

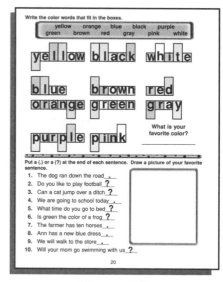

Page 20

Write the color words that fit in the boxes.

yellow   orange   blue   black   purple
green   brown   red   gray   pink   white

yellow   black   white
blue   brown   red
orange   green   gray
purple   pink

What is your favorite color?

Put a (.) or a (?) at the end of each sentence. Draw a picture of your favorite sentence.

1. The dog ran down the road .
2. Do you like to play football ?
3. Can a cat jump over a ditch ?
4. We are going to school today .
5. What time do you go to bed ?
6. Is green the color of a frog ?
7. The farmer has ten horses .
8. Ann has a new blue dress .
9. We will walk to the store .
10. Will your mom go swimming with us ?

20

Grade 1–2   111   **Summer Activities**

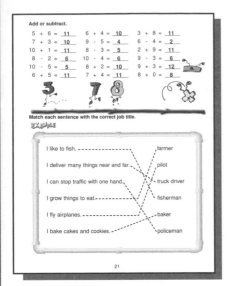

Page 21

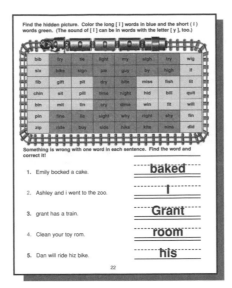

Page 22

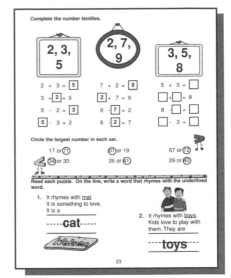

Page 23

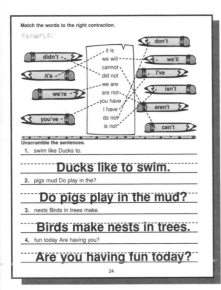

Page 24

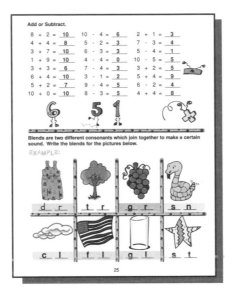

Page 25

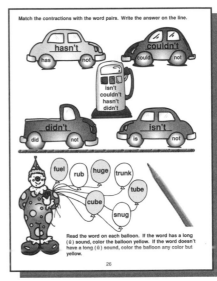

Page 26

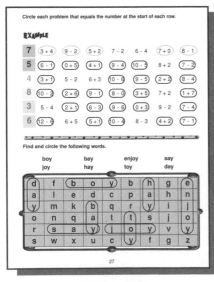

Page 27

Page 28

Page 29

Page 30

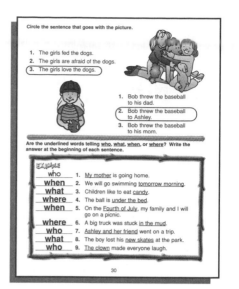

Circle the sentence that goes with the picture.

1. The girls fed the dogs.
2. The girls are afraid of the dogs.
3. (The girls love the dogs.)

1. Bob threw the baseball to his dad.
2. (Bob threw the baseball to Ashley.)
3. Bob threw the baseball to his mom.

Are the underlined words telling who, what, when, or where? Write the answer at the beginning of each sentence.

EXAMPLE
who	1. My mother is going home.
when	2. We will go swimming tomorrow morning.
what	3. Children like to eat candy.
where	4. The ball is under the bed.
when	5. On the Fourth of July, my family and I will go on a picnic.
where	6. A big truck was stuck in the mud.
who	7. Ashley and her friend went on a trip.
what	8. The boy lost his new skates at the park.
who	9. The clown made everyone laugh.

30

Page 31

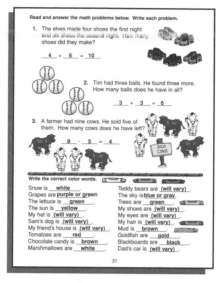

Read and answer the math problems below. Write each problem.

1. The elves made four shoes the first night and six shoes the second night. How many shoes did they make?

   $4 + 6 = 10$

2. Tim had three balls. He found three more. How many balls does he have in all?

   $3 + 3 = 6$

3. A farmer had nine cows. He sold five of them. How many cows does he have left?

   $9 - 5 = 4$

Write the correct color words.

Snow is __white__.
Grapes are __purple or green__.
The lettuce is __green__.
The sun is __yellow__.
My hat is __(will vary)__.
Sam's dog is __(will vary)__.
My friend's house is __(will vary)__.
Tomatoes are __red__.
Chocolate candy is __brown__.
Marshmallows are __white__.

Teddy bears are __(will vary)__.
The sky is __blue or gray__.
Trees are __green__.
My shoes are __(will vary)__.
My eyes are __(will vary)__.
My hair is __(will vary)__.
Mud is __brown__.
Goldfish are __gold__.
Blackboards are __black__.
Dad's car is __(will vary)__.

31

Page 32

Find and circle the words with the long vowel (ū) sound.

use   huge   glue   salute   music
cube   cute   salute   tune

g	l	u	e	l	s	q	t	m
c	a	s	f	r	a	b	u	u
u	o	e	h	t	l	m	n	s
t	d	n	c	h	u	g	e	i
e	j	s	u	k	t	p	v	c
i	w	c	u	b	e	x	e	g

Check the box which best describes the picture.

☐ The mouse is in the box.
☐ The mouse is under the box.
☑ The mouse jumped out of the box.

☐ The bird is sleeping.
☑ The bird loves to sing.
☐ The bird never sings.

32

Page 37

Complete the counting patterns.

| 10 | 20 | 30 | 40 | 50 | 60 | 70 | 80 | 90 | 100 |

| 5 | 10 | 15 | 20 | 25 | 30 | 35 | 40 | 45 | 50 |
| 55 | 60 | 65 | 70 | 75 | 80 | 85 | 90 | 95 | 100 |

| 2 | 4 | 6 | 8 | 10 | 12 | 14 | 16 | 18 | 20 | 22 |
| 24 | 26 | 28 | 30 | 32 | 34 | 36 | 38 | 40 | 42 | 44 |

Write in the short and long vowels.

r a k e   t u b e   b o x   d u c k

t i r e   l a m p   m i l k   t o e

37

Page 38

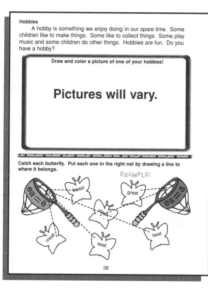

Hobbies

A hobby is something we enjoy doing in our spare time. Some children like to make things. Some like to collect things. Some play music and some children do other things. Hobbies are fun. Do you have a hobby?

Draw and color a picture of one of your hobbies!

Pictures will vary.

Catch each butterfly. Put each one in the right net by drawing a line to where it belongs.

EXAMPLE:

38

Page 39

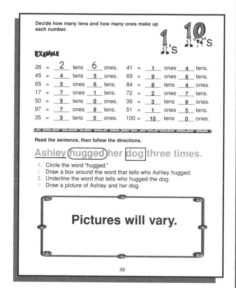

Decide how many tens and how many ones make up each number.

EXAMPLE

26 = __2__ tens __6__ ones.   41 = __1__ ones __4__ tens.
45 = __4__ tens __5__ ones.   69 = __9__ ones __6__ tens.
65 = __5__ tens __6__ ones.   84 = __8__ tens __4__ ones.
17 = __7__ ones __1__ tens.   72 = __2__ ones __7__ tens.
50 = __5__ tens __0__ ones.   39 = __3__ tens __9__ ones.
97 = __7__ ones __9__ tens.   51 = __1__ ones __5__ tens.
35 = __3__ tens __5__ ones.   100 = __10__ tens __0__ ones.

Read the sentence, then follow the directions.

Ashley (hugged) her [dog] three times.

1. Circle the word "hugged."
2. Draw a box around the word that tells who Ashley hugged.
3. Underline the word that tells who hugged the dog.
4. Draw a picture of Ashley and her dog.

Pictures will vary.

39

Page 40

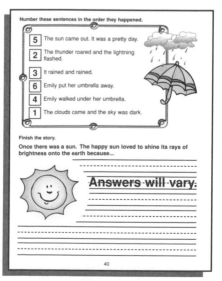

Number these sentences in the order they happened.

5 The sun came out. It was a pretty day.
2 The thunder roared and the lightning flashed.
3 It rained and rained.
6 Emily put her umbrella away.
4 Emily walked under her umbrella.
1 The clouds came and the sky was dark.

Finish the story.

Once there was a sun. The happy sun loved to shine its rays of brightness onto the earth because...

Answers will vary.

40

Page 41

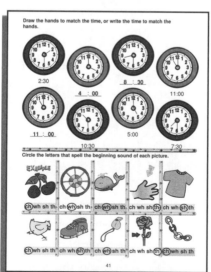

Draw the hands to match the time, or write the time to match the hands.

2:30   8 : 30   11:00

4 : 00   11 : 00   5:00

10:30   7:30

Circle the letters that spell the beginning sound of each picture.

EXAMPLE

ch wh sh th   ch wh sh th   ch wh sh th   ch wh sh th

ch wh sh th   ch wh sh th   ch wh sh th   ch wh sh th

41

Page 42

Read and decide.

One day, a man went on a hunt. He hunted for a long time. At the end of the day, he was very happy. What do you think the man found? Did he find something to eat? Did he find something pretty? Did he find something funny? Decide what the man found and draw a picture of it!

Pictures will vary.

Put the following words in alphabetical order.

he, up, fat, little, big, stop, and, out, slow, go

1. and   6. little
2. big   7. out
3. fat   8. slow
4. go   9. stop
5. he   10. up

42

Page 43

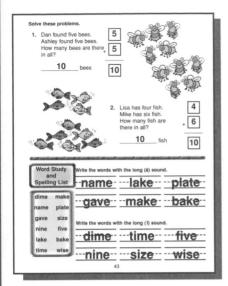

Solve these problems.

1. Dan found five bees. Ashley found five bees. How many bees are there in all?
   5 + 5 = **10** bees | 10

2. Lisa has four fish. Mike has six fish. How many fish are there in all?
   4 + 6 = **10** fish | 10

Word Study and Spelling List	Write the words with the long (ā) sound.
dime make	**name** **lake** **plate**
name plate	**gave** **make** **bake**
gave size	Write the words with the long (ī) sound.
nine five	**dime** **time** **five**
lake bake	**nine** **size** **wise**
time wise	

43

Page 44

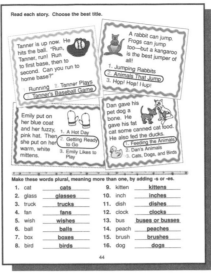

Read each story. Choose the best title.

Tanner is up now. He hits the ball. "Run, Tanner, run! Run to first base, then to second. Can you run to home base?"
1. Running 2. Tanner Plays (Tanner's Baseball Game)

A rabbit can jump. Frogs can jump too—but a kangaroo is the best jumper of all!
1. Jumping Rabbits (2. Animals That Jump) 3. Hop! Hop! I up!

Emily put on her blue coat and her fuzzy, pink hat. Then she put on her warm, white mittens.
1. A Hot Day (2. Getting Ready to Go) 3. Emily Likes to Play

Dan gave his pet dog a bone. He gave his fat cat some canned cat food. He also fed the ducks.
(1. Feeding the Animals) 2. Dan's Animals 3. Cats, Dogs, and Birds

Make these words plural, meaning more than one, by adding -s or -es.

1. cat	**cats**	9. kitten	**kittens**
2. glass	**glasses**	10. inch	**inches**
3. truck	**trucks**	11. dish	**dishes**
4. fan	**fans**	12. clock	**clocks**
5. wish	**wishes**	13. bus	**buses or busses**
6. ball	**balls**	14. peach	**peaches**
7. box	**boxes**	15. brush	**brushes**
8. bird	**birds**	16. dog	**dogs**

44

Page 45

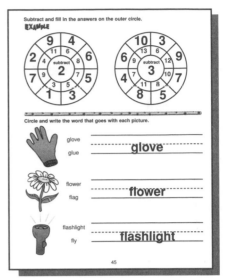

Subtract and fill in the answers on the outer circle.

EXAMPLE

Circle and write the word that goes with each picture.

glove / glue — **glove**

flower / flag — **flower**

flashlight / fly — **flashlight**

45

Page 46

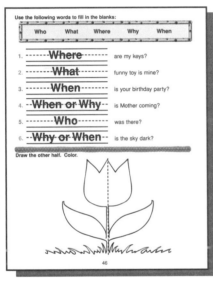

Use the following words to fill in the blanks:

Who   What   Where   Why   When

1. **Where** are my keys?
2. **What** funny toy is mine?
3. **When** is your birthday party?
4. **When or Why** is Mother coming?
5. **Who** was there?
6. **Why or When** is the sky dark?

Draw the other half. Color.

46

Page 47

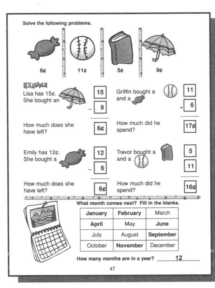

Solve the following problems.

6¢   11¢   5¢   9¢

EXAMPLE
Lisa has 15¢. She bought an [umbrella]. 15 − 9
How much does she have left? 6¢

Griffin bought a [baseball] and a [candy]. 11 + 6
How much did he spend? 17¢

Emily has 12¢. She bought a [candy]. 12 − 6
How much does she have left? 6¢

Trevor bought a [book] and a [baseball]. 5 + 11
How much did he spend? 16¢

What month comes next? Fill in the blanks.

January	February	March
April	May	**June**
July	August	**September**
October	**November**	December

How many months are in a year? **12**

47

Page 48

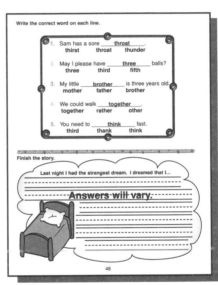

Write the correct word on each line.

1. Sam has a sore **throat**
   thirst   throat   thunder
2. May I please have **three** balls?
   three   third   fifth
3. My little **brother** is three years old.
   mother   father   brother
4. We could walk **together**
   together   rather   other
5. You need to **think** fast.
   third   thank   think

Finish the story.

Last night I had the strangest dream. I dreamed that I... **Answers will vary.**

48

Page 49

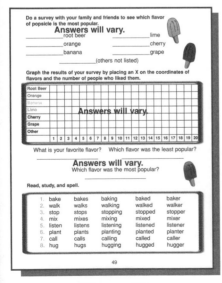

Do a survey with your family and friends to see which flavor of popsicle is the most popular.

Answers will vary.
root beer ___ lime
orange ___ cherry
banana ___ grape
(others not listed)

Graph the results of your survey by placing an X on the coordinates of flavors and the number of people who liked them.

Root Beer				
Orange				
Banana		**Answers will vary.**		
Lime				
Cherry				
Grape				
Other				
1 2 3 4 5 6 7 8 9 10 11 12 13 14 15 16 17 18 19 20

What is your favorite flavor?   Which flavor was the least popular?
Answers will vary.
Which flavor was the most popular?

Read, study, and spell.

1. bake	bakes	baking	baked	baker
2. walk	walks	walking	walked	walker
3. stop	stops	stopping	stopped	stopper
4. mix	mixes	mixing	mixed	mixer
5. listen	listens	listening	listened	listener
6. plant	plants	planting	planted	planter
7. call	calls	calling	called	caller
8. hug	hugs	hugging	hugged	hugger

49

Page 50

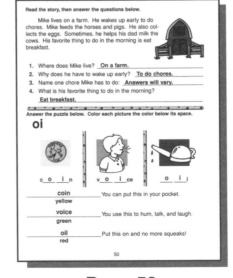

Read the story, then answer the questions below.

Mike lives on a farm. He wakes up early to do chores. Mike feeds the horses and pigs. He also collects the eggs. Sometimes, he helps his dad milk the cows. His favorite thing to do in the morning is eat breakfast.

1. Where does Mike live? **On a farm.**
2. Why does he have to wake up early? **To do chores.**
3. Name one chore Mike has to do: **Answers will vary.**
4. What is his favorite thing to do in the morning? **Eat breakfast.**

Answer the puzzle below. Color each picture the color below its space.

oi

c o i n
coin — yellow — You can put this in your pocket.

v o i ce
voice — green — You use this to hum, talk, and laugh.

o i l
oil — red — Put this on and no more squeaks!

50

Page 51

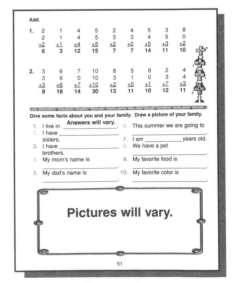

Add.

1. | 2 | 1 | 4 | 5 | 2 | 4 | 5 | 3 | 8 |
    | +2 | +1 | +4 | +5 | +2 | +0 | +5 | +3 | +2 |
    | 6 | 3 | 12 | 15 | 7 | 7 | 14 | 11 | 10 |

2. | 3 | 6 | 7 | 10 | 8 | 5 | 9 | 2 | 4 |
    | 3 | 6 | 0 | 10 | 3 | 1 | 0 | 3 | 4 |
    | +3 | +6 | +7 | +10 | +2 | +5 | +1 | +7 | +3 |
    | 9 | 18 | 14 | 30 | 13 | 11 | 10 | 11 | 11 |

Give some facts about you and your family. Draw a picture of your family.

1. I live in **Answers will vary.**
2. I have ___ sisters.
3. I have ___ brothers.
4. My mom's name is
5. My dad's name is
6. This summer we are going to
7. I am ___ years old.
8. We have a pet
9. My favorite food is
10. My favorite color is

Pictures will vary.

51

Page 52

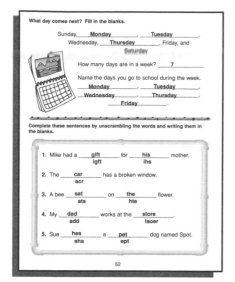

What day comes next? Fill in the blanks.

Sunday, **Monday**, **Tuesday**
Wednesday, **Thursday**, Friday, and
Saturday

How many days are in a week? **7**

Name the days you go to school during the week.
Monday, **Tuesday**,
Wednesday, **Thursday**,
Friday

Complete these sentences by unscrambling the words and writing them in the blanks.

1. Mike had a **gift** for **his** mother. (igft / ihs)
2. The **car** has a broken window. (acr)
3. A bee **sat** on **the** flower. (ats / hte)
4. My **dad** works at the **store**. (add / tsoer)
5. Sue **has** a **pet** dog named Spot. (sha / ept)

52

Page 53

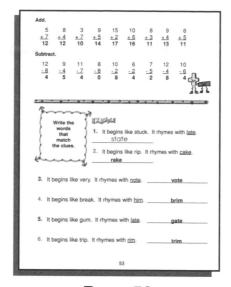

Add.

5 +7 = 12	8 +4 = 12	3 +7 = 10	9 +5 = 14	15 +2 = 17	10 +6 = 16	8 +3 = 11	9 +4 = 13	6 +5 = 11

Subtract.

12 -8 = 4	9 -4 = 5	11 -7 = 4	8 -8 = 0	10 -2 = 8	6 -2 = 4	7 -5 = 2	12 -4 = 8	10 -6 = 4

Write the words that match the clues.

Example
1. It begins like stuck. It rhymes with late. **state**
2. It begins like rip. It rhymes with cake. **rake**
3. It begins like very. It rhymes with note. **vote**
4. It begins like break. It rhymes with him. **brim**
5. It begins like gum. It rhymes with late. **gate**
6. It begins like trip. It rhymes with rim. **trim**

53

Page 54

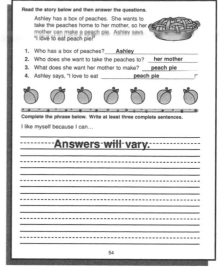

Read the story below and then answer the questions.

Ashley has a box of peaches. She wants to take the peaches home to her mother, so her mother can make a peach pie. Ashley says, "I love to eat peach pie!"

1. Who has a box of peaches? **Ashley**
2. Who does she want to take the peaches to? **her mother**
3. What does she want her mother to make? **peach pie**
4. Ashley says, "I love to eat **peach pie**!"

Complete the phrase below. Write at least three complete sentences.
I like myself because I can...

Answers will vary.

54

Page 55

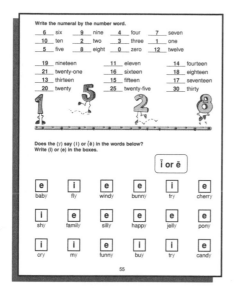

Write the numeral by the number word.

6 six	9 nine	4 four	7 seven
10 ten	2 two	3 three	1 one
5 five	8 eight	0 zero	12 twelve
19 nineteen	11 eleven		14 fourteen
21 twenty-one	16 sixteen		18 eighteen
13 thirteen	15 fifteen		17 seventeen
20 twenty	25 twenty-five		30 thirty

Does the (y) say (i) or (ē) in the words below? Write (i) or (e) in the boxes.

ī or ē

baby e	fly i	windy e	bunny e	fry i	cherry e
shy i	family e	silly e	happy e	jelly e	pony e
cry i	my i	funny e	buy i	try i	candy e

55

Page 56

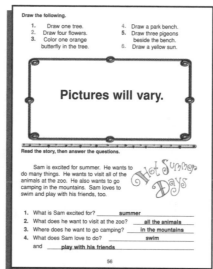

Draw the following.
1. Draw one tree.
2. Draw four flowers.
3. Color one orange butterfly in the tree.
4. Draw a park bench.
5. Draw three pigeons beside the bench.
6. Draw a yellow sun.

Pictures will vary.

Read the story, then answer the questions.

Sam is excited for summer. He wants to do many things. He wants to visit all of the animals at the zoo. He also wants to go camping in the mountains. Sam loves to swim and play with his friends, too.

1. What is Sam excited for? **summer**
2. What does he want to visit at the zoo? **all the animals**
3. Where does he want to go camping? **in the mountains**
4. What does Sam love to do? **swim** and **play with his friends**

56

Page 57

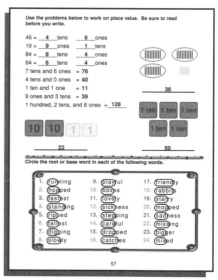

Use the problems below to work on place value. Be sure to read before you write.

46 = **4** tens **6** ones
19 = **9** ones **1** tens
84 = **8** tens **4** ones
64 = **6** tens **4** ones
7 tens and 6 ones = **76**
4 tens and 0 ones = **40**
1 ten and 1 one = **11**
9 ones and 3 tens = **39**
1 hundred, 2 tens, and 8 ones = **128**

36
22   50

Circle the root or base word in each of the following words.

1. running	9. playful	17. friendly
2. hopped	10. boxes	18. rabbits
3. fastest	11. lovely	19. starry
4. standing	12. sickness	20. mopped
5. ripped	13. stepping	21. sadness
6. tallest	14. careful	22. missing
7. digging	15. dropped	23. bigger
8. slowly	16. catches	24. mixed

57

Page 58

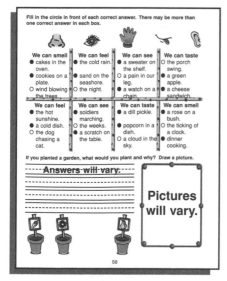

Fill in the circle in front of each correct answer. There may be more than one correct answer in each box.

We can smell
● cakes in the oven.
● cookies on a plate.
O wind blowing in the trees.

We can feel
● the cold rain.
● sand on the seashore.
O the night.

We can see
● a sweater on the shelf.
● a pain in our leg.
● a watch on a chain.

We can taste
O the porch swing.
● a green apple.
● a cheese sandwich.

We can feel
● the hot sunshine.
● a cold dish.
O the dog chasing a cat.

We can see
● soldiers marching.
O the weeks.
● a scratch on the table.

We can taste
● a dill pickle.
● popcorn in a dish.
O a cloud in the sky.

We can smell
● a rose on a bush.
O the ticking of a clock.
● dinner cooking.

If you planted a garden, what would you plant and why? Draw a picture.

Answers will vary.

Pictures will vary.

58

Page 59

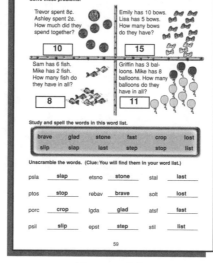

Solve these problems.

Trevor spent 8¢. Ashley spent 2¢. How much did they spend together? **10**

Emily has 10 bows. Lisa has 5 bows. How many bows do they have? **15**

Sam has 6 fish. Mike has 2 fish. How many fish do they have in all? **8**

Griffin has 3 balloons. Mike has 8 balloons. How many balloons do they have in all? **11**

Study and spell the words in this word list.

| brave | glad | stone | fast | crop | lost |
| slip | slap | last | step | stop | list |

Unscramble the words. (Clue: You will find them in your word list.)

psla **slap**   etsno **stone**   stal **last**
ptos **stop**   rebav **brave**   solt **lost**
porc **crop**   lgda **glad**   atsf **fast**
psil **slip**   epst **step**   stil **list**

59

Page 60

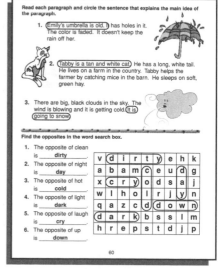

Read each paragraph and circle the sentence that explains the main idea of the paragraph.

1. **Emily's umbrella is old.** It has holes in it. The color is faded. It doesn't keep the rain off her.

2. **Tabby is a tan and white cat.** He has a long, white tail. He lives on a farm in the country. Tabby helps the farmer by catching mice in the barn. He sleeps on soft, green hay.

3. There are big, black clouds in the sky. The wind is blowing and it is getting cold. **It is going to snow.**

Find the opposites in the word search box.
1. The opposite of clean is **dirty**
2. The opposite of night is **day**
3. The opposite of hot is **cold**
4. The opposite of light is **dark**
5. The opposite of laugh is **cry**
6. The opposite of up is **down**

```
v d i r t y e h k
a b a m c e u d g
x c r y o d s a j
w l h o l r j y n
q a z c d d o w n
d a r k b s s l m
h r e p s t d j p
```

60

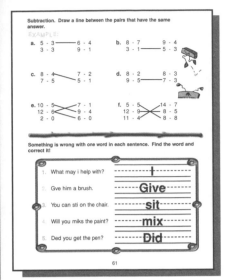

Page 61

Subtraction. Draw a line between the pairs that have the same answer.

EXAMPLE:

a. 5 - 3 —— 6 - 4
   3 - 3 —— 9 - 1

b. 8 - 7 —— 9 - 4
   3 - 1 —— 5 - 3

c. 8 - 4 —— 7 - 5
   7 - 5 —— 5 - 1

d. 8 - 2 —— 8 - 3
   9 - 5 —— 7 - 3

e. 10 - 5 —— 7 - 1
   12 - 6 —— 9 - 4
   2 - 0 —— 6 - 1

f. 5 - 5 —— 14 - 7
   12 - 9 —— 8 - 5
   11 - 4 —— 8 - 8

Something is wrong with one word in each sentence. Find the word and correct it!

1. What may i help with? — I
2. Gve him a brush. — Give
3. You can sti on the chair. — sit
4. Will you miks the paint? — mix
5. Ded you get the pen? — Did

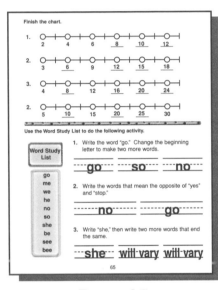

Page 62

Circle the words that do not belong in the numbered lists below.

EXAMPLE

1. beans, carrots, corn, (balls), peas, (books)
2. train, boat, (leg), car, (dress), jet
3. (cat), orange, green, blue, red, (five)
4. lake, ocean, pond, (chair), river, (shoe)
5. bear, (apple), lion, wolf, (pillow), tiger
6. (head), (sleep), jump, hop, run, skip
7. Jane, Kathy, (Tom), (Fred), Jill, Anne
8. (park), scared, happy, sad, mad, (bed)
9. tulip, daffodil, (wagon), daisy, (basket), rose
10. shirt, socks, (bus), (rope), pants, dress

Write a story that begins, "My favorite kind of fruit is _____, because..."

Answers will vary.

Page 63

Help the dogs find their doggy snacks by drawing a line to match each dog with the correct answer bone.

Circle the letters that spell the ending sounds.

EXAMPLE
math
12
-2
10

th sh (ch)   th (sh) ch   th (sh) ch   th sh (ch)   th sh (ch)

th (sh) ch   (th) sh ch   th sh (ch)   (th) sh ch   th sh (ch)

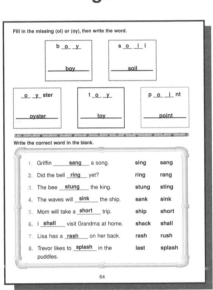

Page 64

Fill in the missing (oi) or (oy), then write the word.

b o y — boy
s o i l — soil
o y ster — oyster
t o y — toy
p o i nt — point

Write the correct word in the blank.

1. Griffin __sang__ a song. (sing, sang)
2. Did the bell __ring__ yet? (ring, rang)
3. The bee __stung__ the king. (stung, sting)
4. The waves will __sink__ the ship. (sank, sink)
5. Mom will take a __short__ trip. (ship, short)
6. I __shall__ visit Grandma at home. (shack, shall)
7. Lisa has a __rash__ on her back. (rash, rush)
8. Trevor likes to __splash__ in the puddles. (last, splash)

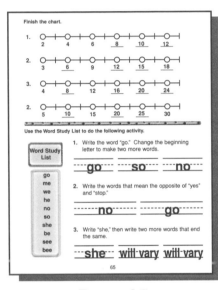

Page 65

Finish the chart.

1. 2 4 6 8 10 12
2. 3 6 9 12 15 18
3. 4 8 12 16 20 24
4. 5 10 15 20 25 30

Use the Word Study List to do the following activity.

Word Study List
go, me, we, he, no, so, she, be, see, bee

1. Write the word "go." Change the beginning letter to make two more words.
   go so no

2. Write the words that mean the opposite of "yes" and "stop."
   no go

3. Write "she," then write two more words that end the same.
   she will vary will vary

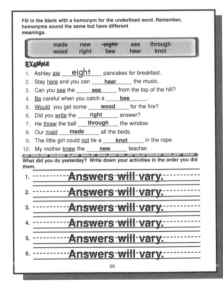

Page 66

Fill in the blank with a homonym for the underlined word. Remember, homonyms sound the same but have different meanings.

made, new, eight, sea, through, wood, right, bee, hear, knot

EXAMPLE
1. Ashley ate __eight__ pancakes for breakfast.
2. Stay here and you can __hear__ the music.
3. Can you see the __sea__ from the top of the hill?
4. Be careful when you catch a __bee__.
5. Would you get some __wood__ for the fire?
6. Did you write the __right__ answer?
7. He threw the ball __through__ the window.
8. Our maid __made__ all the beds.
9. The little girl could not tie a __knot__ in the rope.
10. My mother knew the __new__ teacher.

What did you do yesterday? Write down your activities in the order you did them.

1. Answers will vary.
2. Answers will vary.
3. Answers will vary.
4. Answers will vary.
5. Answers will vary.
6. Answers will vary.

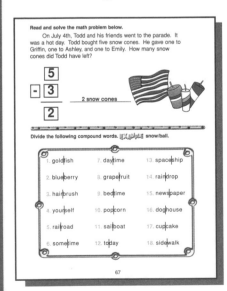

Page 67

Read and solve the math problem below.

On July 4th, Todd and his friends went to the parade. It was a hot day. Todd bought five snow cones. He gave one to Griffin, one to Ashley, and one to Emily. How many snow cones did Todd have left?

5 - 3 = 2   2 snow cones

Divide the following compound words. EXAMPLE snow/ball.

1. gold/fish
2. blue/berry
3. hair/brush
4. your/self
5. rail/road
6. some/time
7. day/time
8. grape/fruit
9. bed/time
10. pop/corn
11. sail/boat
12. to/day
13. space/ship
14. rain/drop
15. news/paper
16. dog/house
17. cup/cake
18. side/walk

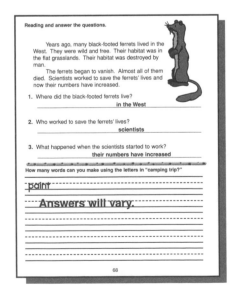

Page 68

Reading and answer the questions.

Years ago, many black-footed ferrets lived in the West. They were wild and free. Their habitat was in the flat grasslands. Their habitat was destroyed by man.

The ferrets began to vanish. Almost all of them died. Scientists worked to save the ferrets' lives and now their numbers have increased.

1. Where did the black-footed ferrets live?
   in the West
2. Who worked to save the ferrets' lives?
   scientists
3. What happened when the scientists started to work?
   their numbers have increased

How many words can you make using the letters in "camping trip?"
paint
Answers will vary.

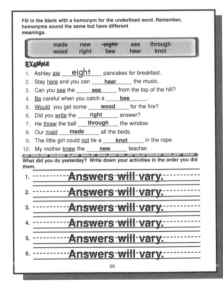

Page 69

Subtraction.

| 10 -2 = 8 | 10 -9 = 1 | 10 -7 = 3 | 10 -1 = 9 | 10 -8 = 2 | 10 -3 = 7 | 10 -4 = 6 | 10 -6 = 4 | 10 -5 = 5 |

| 11 -2 = 9 | 11 -9 = 2 | 11 -7 = 4 | 11 -1 = 10 | 11 -8 = 3 | 11 -3 = 8 | 11 -5 = 6 | 11 -0 = 11 | 11 -6 = 5 |

| 12 -2 = 10 | 12 -9 = 3 | 12 -7 = 5 | 12 -1 = 11 | 12 -8 = 4 | 12 -3 = 9 | 12 -5 = 7 | 12 -0 = 12 | 12 -6 = 6 |

Write a story.

If I were a firecracker, I would...

Answers will vary.

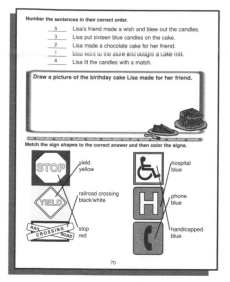

Page 70

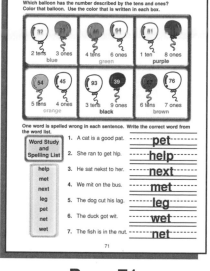

Page 71

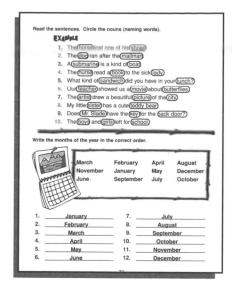

Page 72

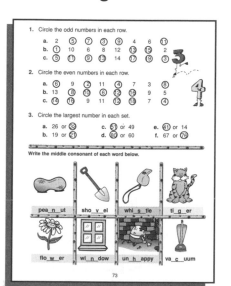

Page 73

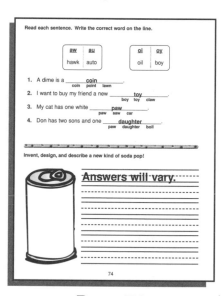

Page 74

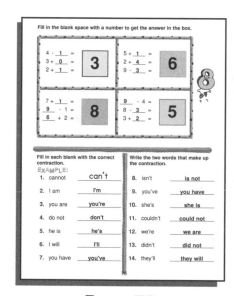

Page 75

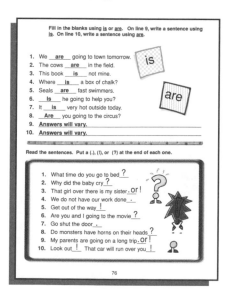

Page 76

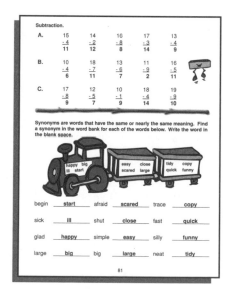

Page 81

Page 82

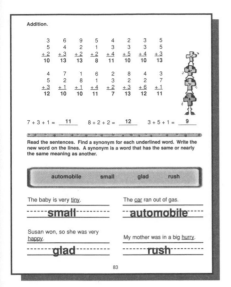

Page 83

Addition.

3	6	9	5	4	2	3	5
5	4	2	1	3	3	3	5
+2	+3	+2	+2	+4	+5	+4	+3
10	13	13	8	11	10	10	13

4	7	1	6	2	8	4	3
5	2	8	1	3	2	2	7
+3	+1	+1	+4	+2	+3	+6	+1
12	10	10	11	7	13	12	11

7 + 3 + 1 = __11__   8 + 2 + 2 = __12__   3 + 5 + 1 = __9__

Read the sentences. Find a synonym for each underlined word. Write the new word on the lines. A synonym is a word that has the same or nearly the same meaning as another.

automobile   small   glad   rush

The baby is very tiny.
__small__

The car ran out of gas.
__automobile__

Susan won, so she was very happy.
__glad__

My mother was in a big hurry.
__rush__

Page 84

Make an (X) by the answers to the questions.

How is a snake like a turtle?
1. They both have shells.
_X_ 2. They both can be found on land.
_X_ 3. They are both reptiles.
4. They both fly in the sky.
_X_ 5. They both have tails.
6. They both eat flies.
7. They both have legs.

How is a bike like a truck?
_X_ 1. They both have tires.
2. They both need gas.
_X_ 3. They can be different colors.
_X_ 4. They can both be new and shiny.
5. They both have four wheels.
_X_ 6. They both can go.
7. You can ride in both of them.

How is a sailor like a doctor?
_X_ 1. They both wear white.
2. They both wear hats.
3. They both work with dogs.
_X_ 4. They both are people.
5. Their job is to help sick people.
6. They have to work on a ship.
_X_ 7. They both should be helpful.

Finish the story.
One day Ashley went out to play. Her friend, Lisa, was already outside.
Lisa said to Ashley, "Let's go play…"

__Answers will vary.__

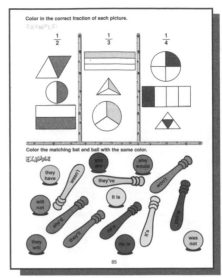

Page 85

Color in the correct fraction of each picture.
EXAMPLE:
½   ⅓   ¼

Color the matching bat and ball with the same color.
EXAMPLE

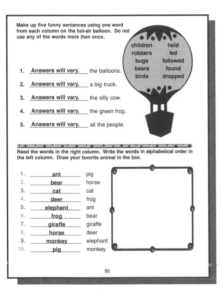

Page 86

Make up five funny sentences using one word from each column on the hot-air balloon. Do not use any of the words more than once.

children   held
robbers   fed
bugs   followed
bears   found
birds   dropped

1. __Answers will vary.__ the balloons.
2. __Answers will vary.__ a big truck.
3. __Answers will vary.__ the silly cow.
4. __Answers will vary.__ the green frog.
5. __Answers will vary.__ all the people.

Read the words in the right column. Write the words in alphabetical order in the left column. Draw your favorite animal in the box.

	left	right
1.	ant	pig
2.	bear	horse
3.	cat	cat
4.	deer	frog
5.	elephant	ant
6.	frog	bear
7.	giraffe	giraffe
8.	horse	deer
9.	monkey	elephant
10.	pig	monkey

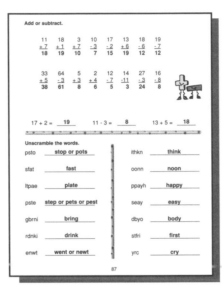

Page 87

Add or subtract.

11	18	3	10	17	13	18	19
+7	+1	+7	-3	-2	+6	-6	-7
18	19	10	7	15	19	12	12

33	64	5	2	12	14	27	16
+5	-3	+3	+4	-7	-11	-3	-8
38	61	8	6	5	3	24	8

17 + 2 = __19__   11 - 3 = __8__   13 + 5 = __18__

Unscramble the words.

psto	__stop or pots__	ithkn	__think__
sfat	__fast__	oonn	__noon__
ltpae	__plate__	ppayh	__happy__
pste	__step or pets or pest__	seay	__easy__
gbrni	__bring__	dbyo	__body__
rdnki	__drink__	stfri	__first__
enwt	__went or newt__	yrc	__cry__

Page 88

Read the words aloud, then write them in alphabetical order.

rabbit, snake, lion, dog, fish, dish, make, candy, puppy, vase

1.	__candy__	6.	__make__
2.	__dish__	7.	__puppy__
3.	__dog__	8.	__rabbit__
4.	__fish__	9.	__snake__
5.	__lion__	10.	__vase__

Dairy designs. A dairy company has asked you to create a design for a milk carton. Create and color an original milk carton design for the company.

__Pictures will vary.__

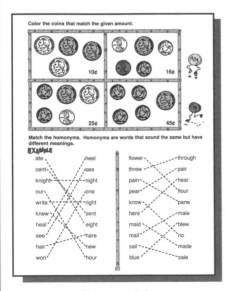

Page 89

Color the coins that match the given amount.

10¢   16¢   25¢   45¢

Match the homonyms. Homonyms are words that sound the same but have different meanings.
EXAMPLE

ate — heel
cent — sea
knight — night
our — one
write — right
knew — sent
heal — eight
see — hare
hair — new
won — hour

flower — through
threw — pair
pain — hear
pear — flour
know — pane
here — male
maid — blew
mail — no
sail — made
blue — sale

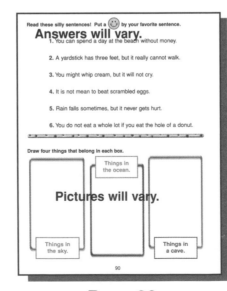

Page 90

Read these silly sentences! Put a ☺ by your favorite sentence.

__Answers will vary.__

1. You can spend a day at the beach without money.
2. A yardstick has three feet, but it really cannot walk.
3. You might whip cream, but it will not cry.
4. It is not mean to beat scrambled eggs.
5. Rain falls sometimes, but it never gets hurt.
6. You do not eat a whole lot if you eat the hole of a donut.

Draw four things that belong in each box.

Things in the ocean.
Things in the sky.
Things in a cave.

__Pictures will vary.__

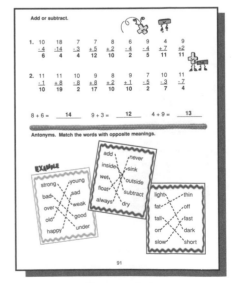

Page 91

Add or subtract.

1.
10	18	7	7	8	6	9	4
-4	-14	-3	+5	+2	-4	+7	+2
6	4	4	12	11	2	5	11	11

2.
11	11	10	9	8	9	7	10	11
-1	+8	-8	+8	+2	+1	-5	-3	-7
10	19	2	17	10	10	2	7	4

8 + 6 = __14__   9 + 3 = __12__   4 + 9 = __13__

Antonyms. Match the words with opposite meanings.
EXAMPLE

strong — young
bad — sad
over — weak
old — good
happy — under

add — never
inside — sink
wet — outside
float — subtract
always — dry

light — thin
fat — off
tall — fast
on — dark
slow — short

Page 92

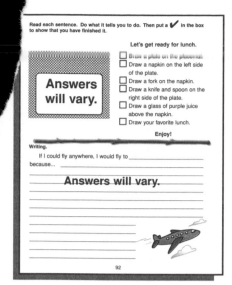

Read each sentence. Do what it tells you to do. Then put a ✔ in the box to show that you have finished it.

Let's get ready for lunch.

☐ Draw a plate on the placemat.
☐ Draw a napkin on the left side of the plate.
☐ Draw a fork on the napkin.
☐ Draw a knife and spoon on the right side of the plate.
☐ Draw a glass of purple juice above the napkin.
☐ Draw your favorite lunch.

Answers will vary.

Enjoy!

Writing.

If I could fly anywhere, I would fly to _____ because...

Answers will vary.

92

Page 93

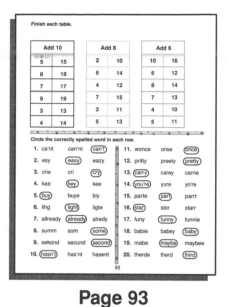

Finish each table.

Add 10	
5	15
8	18
7	17
9	19
3	13
4	14

Add 8	
2	10
6	14
4	12
7	15
3	11
5	13

Add 6	
10	16
6	12
8	14
7	13
4	10
5	11

Circle the correctly spelled word in each row.

1. ca'nt can'nt (can't)
2. esy (easy) eazy
3. crie cri (cry)
4. kea (key) kee
5. (buy) buye biy
6. lihg (light) ligte
7. allready (already) alredy
8. summ som (some)
9. sekond secund (second)
10. (hasn't) has'nt hasent
11. wonce onse (once)
12. pritty preety (pretty)
13. (carry) carey carrie
14. (you're) yure yo're
15. parte (part) parrt
16. (star) stor starr
17. funy (funny) funnie
18. babie babey (baby)
19. mabe (maybe) maybee
20. therde therd (third)

93

Page 94

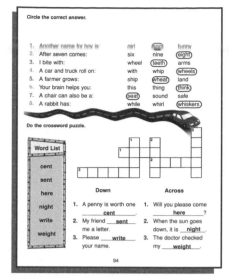

Circle the correct answer.

1. Another name for boy is: girl (man) funny
2. After seven comes: six nine (eight)
3. I bite with: wheel (teeth) arms
4. A car and truck roll on: with whip (wheels)
5. A farmer grows: ship (wheat) land
6. Your brain helps you: this thing (think)
7. A chair can also be a: (seat) sound safe
8. A rabbit has: while whirl (whiskers)

Do the crossword puzzle.

Word List

cent
sent
here
night
write
weight

Down

1. A penny is worth one ____ **cent**.
2. My friend ____ **sent** me a letter.
3. Please ____ **write** your name.

Across

1. Will you please come ____ **here** ?
2. When the sun goes down, it is ____ **night** .
3. The doctor checked my ____ **weight** .

94

Page 95

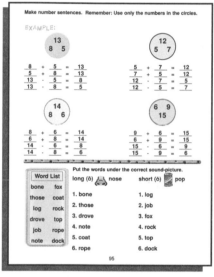

Make number sentences. Remember: Use only the numbers in the circles.

EXAMPLE:

(13 8 5)

8 + 5 = 13
5 + 8 = 13
13 - 5 = 8
13 - 8 = 5

(12 5 7)

5 + 7 = 12
7 + 5 = 12
12 - 7 = 5
12 - 5 = 7

(14 8 6)

8 + 6 = 14
6 + 8 = 14
14 - 6 = 8
14 - 8 = 6

(6 9 15)

9 + 6 = 15
6 + 9 = 15
15 - 6 = 9
15 - 9 = 6

Put the words under the correct sound-picture.

Word List
bone fox
those coat
log rock
drove top
job rope
note dock

long (ō) nose
1. bone
2. those
3. drove
4. note
5. coat
6. rope

short (ŏ) pop
1. log
2. job
3. fox
4. rock
5. top
6. dock

95

Page 96

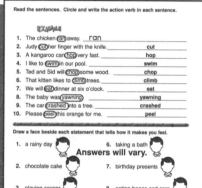

Read the sentences. Circle and write the action verb in each sentence.

EXAMPLE

1. The chicken (ran) away. ran
2. Judy (cut) her finger with the knife. cut
3. A kangaroo can (hop) very fast. hop
4. I like to (swim) in our pool. swim
5. Ted and Sid will (chop) some wood. chop
6. That kitten likes to (climb) trees. climb
7. We will (eat) dinner at six o'clock. eat
8. The baby was (yawning). yawning
9. The car (crashed) into a tree. crashed
10. Please (peel) this orange for me. peel

Draw a face beside each statement that tells how it makes you feel.

1. a rainy day
2. chocolate cake
3. playing soccer
4. camping in the mountains
5. fighting with a friend
6. taking a bath
7. birthday presents
8. eating beans and corn
9. catching a fly ball
10. going to Grandmother's

Answers will vary.

96

Page 97

Add.

1. 3 3 2 4 5 7 3
    2 4 1 2 3 4 1 5
   +1 +2 +2 +3 +3 +6 +2 +4
    6 9 9 7 10 15 10 12

2. 2 1 6 7 4 5 4 8 4
    3 3 2 5 2 4 1 6
   +2 +6 +1 +1 +2 +3 +1 +2 +3
    6 10 10 11 10 9 11 13

Write soft (c) words under pencil. Write hard (c) words under candy.

grocery cattle cement corn price
cake cellar crib grace cow

pencil
1. grocery
2. cellar
3. cement
4. grace
5. price

candy
1. cake
2. cattle
3. crib
4. corn
5. cow

97

Page 98

Unscramble the sentences. Write the words in the correct order.

1. sun shine will today The.

The sun will shine today.

2. mile today I a walked.

I walked a mile today.

3. house We painted our.

We painted our house.

4. Mother knit will I something for.

I will knit something for Mother.

Write a letter. Ask someone to a silly picnic.
Start your letter with "Dear _____:
End your letter with "Yours truly, _____:

Answers will vary.

98

Page 99

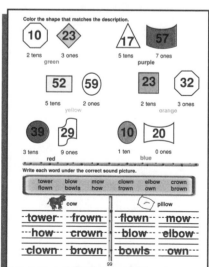

Color the shape that matches the description.

10 23 17 57
2 tens 3 ones 5 tens 7 ones
green purple

52 59 23 32
5 tens 2 ones 2 tens 3 ones
yellow orange

39 29 10 20
3 tens 9 ones 1 ten 0 ones
red blue

Write each word under the correct sound picture.

tower blow mow clown elbow crown
flown bowls how frown own brown

cow
tower frown
how crown
clown brown

pillow
flown mow
blow elbow
bowls own

99

Page 100

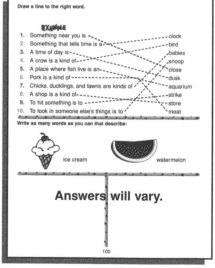

Draw a line to the right word.

EXAMPLE

1. Something near you is — close
2. Something that tells time is a — clock
3. A time of day is — dusk
4. A crow is a kind of — bird
5. A place where fish live is an — aquarium
6. Pork is a kind of — meat
7. Chicks, ducklings, and fawns are kinds of — babies
8. A shop is a kind of — store
9. To hit something is to — strike
10. To look in someone else's things is to — snoop

Write as many words as you can that describe:

ice cream   watermelon

Answers will vary.

100

Page 101

Subtract.

57	68	96	57	38	59	64	77	54
-32	-44	-92	-43	-3	-45	-42	-34	-20
25	24	4	14	35	14	22	43	34

83	75	48	95	68	39	89	93	69
-62	-4	-4	-31	-26	-10	-53	-10	-35
21	55	44	64	42	29	36	83	34

19	24	52	63	76	88	90	71	29
-3	-11	-31	-41	-22	-44	-30	-51	-15
16	13	21	22	54	44	60	20	14

Write in the name of each picture and color.

so c k   gr a ss   'f i sh

sh i rt   s t ove   gat e

101

Page 102

Read each sentence. Do what it tells you to do. Then put a ✔ in the box to show that you have finished it.

Let's go to the park and play.

☐ Draw a swingset.
☐ Draw a slide.
☐ Draw a sandpile.
☐ Draw green grass.
☐ Draw one apple tree.
☐ Draw a yellow sun in the sky.
☐ Draw a blue sky.

Pictures will vary.

Have fun!

Before school starts again, I want to...

Answers will vary.

102

Page 103

Finish each table.
EXAMPLE

subtract 5	
9	4
5	0
7	2
10	5
11	6
8	3

subtract 3	
10	7
9	6
7	4
8	5
9	6
11	8

subtract 2	
11	9
7	5
9	7
5	3
8	6
6	4

Circle the right (r) controlled vowel.
EXAMPLE   b(ir)d

103

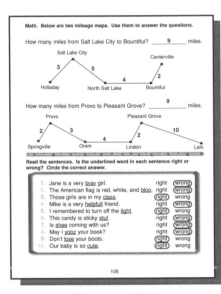

Page 104

Complete the riddles.

1. I am rather tiny. I have wings and buzz around. I can be a real pest at picnics. I am a _____ **bee** _____.

2. I was just born. My mother and father feed me and keep me dry. I cry, and sleep, but I cannot walk. I am a _____ **baby** _____.

3. I am made of metal and am quite little. I can lock things up and open them, too! I am a _____ **key** _____.

4. I like to sing. I lay eggs. I like to eat bugs and worms. I am a _____ **bird** _____.

Write a story about spiders.

Answers will vary.

104

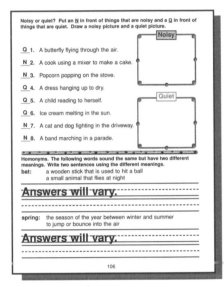

Page 105

Math. Below are two mileage maps. Use them to answer the questions.

How many miles from Salt Lake City to Bountiful? _____ 9 _____ miles.

Salt Lake City   Centerville
3   5   4   2
Holladay   North Salt Lake   Bountiful

How many miles from Provo to Pleasant Grove? _____ 9 _____ miles.

Provo   Pleasant Grove
2   3   4   2   10
Springville   Orem   Lindon   Lehi

Read the sentences. Is the underlined word in each sentence right or wrong? Circle the correct answer.

1. Jane is a very brav girl.   right (wrong)
2. The American flag is red, white, and bloo.   right (wrong)
3. Those girls are in my class.   (right) wrong
4. Mike is a very helpfull friend.   (right) wrong
5. I remembered to turn off the light.   (right) wrong
6. This candy is sticky stuf.   right (wrong)
7. Is shee coming with us?   right (wrong)
8. May I yooz your book?   right (wrong)
9. Don't lose your boots.   (right) wrong
10. Our baby is so cute.   (right) wrong

105

Page 106

Noisy or quiet? Put an N in front of things that are noisy and a Q in front of things that are quiet. Draw a noisy picture and a quiet picture.

Q 1. A butterfly flying through the air.
N 2. A cook using a mixer to make a cake.
N 3. Popcorn popping on the stove.
Q 4. A dress hanging up to dry.
Q 5. A child reading to herself.
Q 6. Ice cream melting in the sun.
N 7. A cat and dog fighting in the driveway.
N 8. A band marching in a parade.

Noisy

Quiet

Homonyms. The following words sound the same but have two different meanings. Write two sentences using the different meanings.

bat: a wooden stick that is used to hit a ball
a small animal that flies at night

Answers will vary.

spring: the season of the year between winter and summer
to jump or bounce into the air

Answers will vary.

106